*The*
# Everyday
## *empath*

© Forrest Hardin

## About the Author

**Raven Digitalis** (Missoula, MT) is the author of *Esoteric Empathy* and a number of metaphysical titles published by Llewellyn. He is a Neopagan Priest and cofounder of an Eastern Hellenistic nonprofit multicultural Pagan temple called Opus Aima Obscuræ (OAO). Also trained in Eastern philosophies, Raven has been an earth-based practitioner since 1999, a Priest since 2003, a Freemason since 2012, and an empath all his life. He holds a degree in anthropology from the University of Montana and is also a professional tarot reader, DJ, small-scale farmer, small-scale card magician, and animal rights advocate. Visit Raven at:

www.ravendigitalis.com
www.facebook.com/ravendigitalis
www.opusaimaobscurae.org
www.facebook.com/opusaimaobscurae

# The
# Everyday
# *empath*

### achieve
### *energetic balance*
### in your life

Llewellyn Publications
Woodbury, Minnesota

First Edition
Third Printing, 2021

Cover design by Shira Atakpu

Llewellyn Publications is a registered trademark of Llewellyn Worldwide Ltd.

**Library of Congress Cataloging-in-Publication Data**

Names: Digitalis, Raven, author.
Title: The everyday empath : achieve energetic balance in your life / by
    Raven Digitalis.
Description: Woodbury, Minnesota : Llewellyn Worldwide, [2019] | Includes
    bibliographical references.
Identifiers: LCCN 2018055803 (print) | LCCN 2018059923 (ebook) | ISBN
    9780738758640 (ebook) | ISBN 9780738758602 (alk. paper)
Subjects: LCSH: Empathy. | Sensitivity (Personality trait)
Classification: LCC BF575.E55 (ebook) | LCC BF575.E55 D54 2019 (print) |
DDC
    152.4/1—dc23
LC record available at https://lccn.loc.gov/2018055803

Llewellyn Publications
A Division of Llewellyn Worldwide Ltd.
2143 Wooddale Drive
Woodbury, MN 55125-2989
www.llewellyn.com

Printed in the United States of America

# Other Books by Raven Digitalis

*Esoteric Empathy*
(Llewellyn, 2016)

*Goth Craft*
(Llewellyn, 2007)

*Shadow Magick Compendium*
(Llewellyn, 2008)

*Planetary Spells & Rituals*
(Llewellyn, 2010)

*For Estha K. V. McNevin and William F. L. Richardson,*
*my two greatest teachers of empathy.*

*And for he who is on his way…*

*777*

# Contents

# Exercises

# Everyday Empathic Techniques

# Introduction

Greetings, beloved reader! Thank you for picking up a copy of this book. My guess is that you either identify as an empath, wonder if you might be one, or are trying to understand someone in your life who demonstrates a high level of empathy. Whatever the case, this book is designed to help sensitive readers learn to achieve energetic balance in daily life. This book provides information, perspectives, and techniques for enriching your life with the gift of empathy.

Personally, I've been an empath all my life. Like any other gift (and yes, it *is* a gift!), empathy is an ability that everyone has to one degree or another. It's not only a spiritual ability; it's also very much biological. Empathy makes the world go round because if we can truly understand each other's perspectives, we can begin to evolve socially. In fact, it is generally accepted by the scientific community that empathy itself is connected to the evolution of our species. By cooperating and supporting one another, humankind can more easily advance as a whole.

In my teenage years, I discovered that there was a term for my tendency to absorb and "take on" the emotions of others around me. Truth be told, we are all developing empaths—and thank goodness for that!

I've long felt a calling to explore what it means to be highly empathic, especially during times of emotional turmoil. At the end of the day, the biggest recommendation I have for struggling empaths is to explore the concept of *selfless service*. I've long believed that part of an empath's calling is to help others through life's journey. This is why I write metaphysical books, in addition to providing spiritual consultations, working with individuals with disabilities, and co-operating a nonprofit multicultural temple and farm. Empaths of all stripes can find personal healing simply by assisting and uplifting others to the best of their ability.

It feels good to give back. For empaths who seek emotional equilibrium within themselves and their environment, there is no better feeling in the world than to realize that we can have a significant positive influence on those around us. This book will explore these themes alongside the most important theme of them all: personal balance.

When we constantly and consistently seek emotional balance in our own lives, we become better equipped to help others on an emotional level. Individuals who identify as empaths *feel* the intricacies of life on a very deep level. We are emotionally invested in all of life's experiences because that's just how we're wired. We can lead by example by utilizing techniques that keep us centered and healthy.

*The Everyday Empath* is a book for everyone. It encompasses a broad range of empathetic approaches and does not assume that the reader follows any specific spiritual path. The first metaphysical books I wrote were focused on Wicca, Paganism, and magickal spirituality. In fact, my original book on the subject of empathy, called *Esoteric Empathy*, focuses greatly on these metaphysical aspects.

Regardless of your own spiritual approach, this book will help you gain perspectives that can be of assistance on your own empathic expedition. In these pages, you will discover numerous approaches to the experience of empathy. This is designed to give readers a well-rounded view of what it means to experience high levels of empathy in daily life. From science to spirituality, this book emphasizes the necessity for personal balance in order to live an empathically empowered life.

Just the same, I've got to be totally honest here: Even if I were to compile an enormous tome consisting of all the empathic information in the world, it still wouldn't be enough. The material presented here, and indeed in all empathic studies, is but a collection of tools to help you along the way. The true path of achieving energetic balance comes from discovering what works best for you in life and choosing to actively apply those skills throughout your daily experience.

Empathy doesn't always feel good. Sometimes it might seem like life would be easier if we weren't so highly sensitive and even persuadable. This book provides techniques, ideas, and practices that can make everyday empathic challenges a bit easier to manage. If we can learn to control our abilities, we can more easily function in daily life without becoming completely overwhelmed.

There are numerous methods empaths can employ to maintain emotional equilibrium. By intentionally studying the physiology, psychology, and metaphysics of empathy, we can gain a more well-rounded and objective view of what we're working with. The world needs us. The time for global empathy is now.

As you read the pages of this book, try thinking about experiences in your life that have solidified in your mind the fact that you are more empathic than average. It's likely that you discovered this book because you want to better understand your empathic nature and learn how to utilize this powerful gift for the greater good.

The information presented here is meant to act as a bridge between empathic cluelessness and deeper emotional study. This is an introductory-style book for those who are just discovering that they identify as an empath. This book can also be useful for individuals who are trying to understand highly empathic friends, family members, colleagues, or clients. Whatever the case, it is my hope that this book helps enrich your own empathic journey and provides a springboard for further study.

I encourage you to come to your own conclusions and to research additional information on some of the topics presented in this book. Only by applying this information to your life can you truly enrich your empathic experience and discover what works best for you personally when approaching reality with a high level of emotional sensitivity. I am right here alongside you on this journey of a lifetime.

It not only is possible but is commendable to live an empathetic life while working toward achieving holistic personal balance. Sometimes we just need guides along the path to point the way and encourage our development. As we grow in our empathic understanding, it becomes our duty to do the same for others along the way. So without further adieu, let's dive into the waters of empathic understanding.

**Exercise:** *A Public Empathic Experiment*

Empathy is afoot everywhere. It can be a rewarding experience to see empathy in action in various situations around us. In order to better understand empathy, it's a good idea to see it playing out in a variety of scenarios.

It's easy to get caught up in our own empathic experiences. However, it's essential to maintain a more objective view of empathy throughout our own subjective experiences. We can become more objective about empathy by observing it in others rather than just ourselves. When we observe and take note of examples of empathy around us, we put ourselves in the position of student, ready and eager to learn about the world.

Highly empathic people have a uniquely "pure" side. This isn't to say that we can't be selfish pricks, because we certainly can at times. It's vital for us to hold on to our pure, childlike, curious side if we wish to thrive as spiritual individuals, regardless of the curveballs life throws in our direction. When we observe others experiencing different levels of empathy, we once again become the student, a curious observer who wishes to learn about the world.

For readers who are drawn to the tarot, I recommend meditating on the Fool card of your favorite deck. Unlike the Fool, who is unaware of the hidden danger before him, you have a keen awareness of the social benefits and challenges of the empathic experience. The Fool is bright-eyed and bushy-tailed, ready to embrace the mystery of life and discover his place in the workings of the universe. This holy Fool represents innocent and uncontaminated aspects of our humanity, and these aspects are ideal to draw upon when we find ourselves in learning situations.

For this exercise, you will deliberately observe empathy in social situations. For this purpose, allow yourself to be as emotionally unaffected as possible. In order to see empathy demonstrated in others' lives and to cultivate a more objective view of it ourselves, we must separate ourselves emotionally and simply *observe*.

Set some time aside to people-watch in various situations and environments. Take a journal with you and write down your observations. Remember, it is your job to become the observer, not the observed, so if you must do a little fake "writing" or pretend to be engrossed in a phone conversation, that's okay. In this exercise, it is your job to step out of your own mind, discreetly observe, and secretly report.

Keep in mind that you're not doing anything wrong. Most people would agree that it's not unethical to observe or even scrutinize people in public situations. When we are in public, we should expect to be observed and assessed to some degree—something that is particularly challenging for empaths who deal with social anxiety. It is not wrong for us to observe and take note of emotional exchanges between individuals in public settings.

1. Find a location with heavy foot traffic, such as a mall or shopping center, locate a comfortable place to sit, and begin writing in your journal. Take note of various individuals who are interacting together, paying particular attention to emotional exchanges. Make note of the various people you are briefly observing, even if it's written in shorthand, such as "Woman, 40ish + boy, 10ish." From there, note the specific emotional exchanges occurring.

2. Take notes. Following the previous example, you might write something like this: "Child wants to visit ice cream shop. Mom gives polite no. Child gets mad. Mom also gets

mad/stern. Mom tells child why no ice cream. Child is still upset, no longer irate. Both frustrated, walk away." In this example, you are able to observe that the child's desire created an emotional interaction between himself and the parent. The mother drew a boundary rather than getting sucked into the emotion. In other words, the mother utilized rational cognition to stop the emotion from spreading. The child was upset by this boundary because he could not fully understand the rationale behind it. From there, they empathically absorbed each other's emotions and walked away with only a few ruffled feathers.

3. Continue this process with various other groups of people. Because it is likely that many of these individuals will be walking on their way to a destination, many of the exchanges are likely to be brief. Try not to follow any of your "subjects" unless it feels right and you won't be noticed—just don't be a creeper! Because many of these observations will be brief, writing in shorthand is a wise idea. Don't feel obligated to observe everyone you see; be selective about your subjects.

4. Throughout this exercise, it's a good idea to observe different types of people and see how they interact with each other emotionally. From there, you can observe how empathy functions among different people at various levels. You are also likely to encounter a number of people having a conversation on their cell phone. This creates an interesting dynamic where you are able to accurately observe only one solitary person. In this situation, it may be ideal to take note of their body language and facial expressions (assuming you are able to regularly glance up from your journal without being

spotted as an observer). If you encounter solitary individuals or individuals who do not appear to be interacting with others, don't bother noting them because this empathic study is aimed at observing how people interact socially with one another and how empathy fits into the equation from party to party.

5. Take note specifically of how and where you witness emotional contagion taking place. Do you see someone becoming affected by the emotion of another person? How does this play out, and between whom does it happen? Which subjects do you believe are overreacting in any given situation, and which subjects do you feel are underreacting? Do you feel that some individuals appear socially dominant while others appear more submissive? Do most of the individuals appear to be on the same wavelength, or do you notice disarray in most parties? Try not to second-guess your observations and notes; they are for you to analyze at a later time.

6. You might consider taking this show on the road. Try observing people in other social situations, like at a play or movie theater or maybe at a beach or by a lakeside. How do different environments seem to influence social interactions? Most importantly, what did you learn from this experience and how will these observations influence your own social interactions?

chapter one

# What Is Empathy, Anyway?

*Empathy* is a term that has gained widespread popularity in the twenty-first century. Believe it or not, the word *empathy* in the English language is actually less than a hundred years old! The term comes from the German *Einfühlung*, meaning "feeling into," and refers to experiencing an external emotion as if it were one's own. Empathy is a sort of emotional internalization, unlike sympathy, which is more mental or cognitive.

A related self-identifying term, *empath*, gained public recognition in the sixties—thanks largely to characters on *Star Trek*! The term was first used clinically in the realm of psychotherapy by Karla McLaren, who has written some of the most helpful books about empathy available. (See the further reading list at the end of this book.)

We exist in a period of time that is witnessing a surge of empathic studies. With each passing day, new information about empathy is researched and reported on from a variety of scientific and metaphysical angles. It is truly amazing to see professionals of all varieties learning the value of empathy and applying it directly to their work.

One example of this integration that stands out to me is within cultural anthropology and sociology. Being that I studied these disciplines in college, I find it beautiful to see an increased emphasis on the need for empathy when studying other people and cultures. During the early developmental phases of these social studies, the Western observer was seen as an outsider who had come to document the "other." Modern anthropologists and sociologists recognize the limitations of this divisive approach, not to mention the judgments that come along with it. When empathy is activated in social fieldwork, the anthropologist or sociologist becomes an active participant rather than a mere observer.

Experiencing empathy with others is a mark of trust. Empathy implies some degree of vulnerability, because the experience allows external emotions to enter one's sphere of experience and vice versa. Empathy is considerate, compassionate, and engaging. Empathy itself also suggests that emotions of all types are both valid and important; this wisdom can go a long way in encouraging the world to be a softer, kinder, and safer place.

## Social Aspects of Empathy

Empathy is everywhere. In many ways, empathy is the social glue that holds us all together. Empathy is a social experience that involves feeling external emotional energy to the point of *mirroring* an emotion and taking it into one's own experience. Empathy can be seen as feeling *as* the other, while sympathy, on the other hand, can be seen as feeling *for* the other. In daily life, an emotionally healthy person will experience both empathy and sympathy to varying degrees.

When a person has an empathic experience, they are transcending sympathy by actually *absorbing* or *stepping into* an emotional frequency. This empathic energy can come from another person, a group of people, an animal, a film or play, a story in the news, or even the emotional energy in an environment.

Everyone is empathic to one degree or another, and when a person has their empathetic receptors turned on "high," it can be an extremely overwhelming experience. This is why it is so important to understand the experience of empathy and to learn techniques to help keep us socially balanced and emotionally healthy.

Empathy directly implies emotion. We are all emotional beings, and we all deserve to have positive emotional experiences in order to function in life with happiness and health. Our own emotional wellness greatly determines how we react to life's ups and downs. Many spiritual people say that these responses also affect our karma. The knowledge of this link between emotional health and karma evokes a sense of personal responsibility to maintain our own emotional health.

### Everyday Empathic Techniques

Individuals with high levels of empathy are likely to identify with a number of the following qualities. Although everyone experiences different types of empathic processing, those who are strongly empathetic have a number of things in common. If you identify with many of these points, congratulate yourself on being a member of the world's empathic family!

- **Emotional absorption:** This is the experience of absorbing surrounding emotions. This makes it challenging to distinguish between our own emotions and those of other people.

Empaths must work especially hard at differentiating between internal and external emotions on a daily basis.

- **Understanding other perspectives:** Highly empathic individuals have the ability to understand the reasons behind other people's perspectives. Even if the empath does not feel the same way as the other person, it's almost effortless for them to step into the viewpoint of someone else in order to see where they're coming from. When the situation is approached with self-awareness, the empath can understand the other without necessarily "taking on" their perceptions as if they were their own. We can choose to understand and relate to others while still retaining our own identity and perspectives.

- **Gullibility:** Empaths are notoriously gullible. If a person is projecting a certain emotion, the empath is likely to feel that emotion and believe it to be real. This is the main reason why empathic individuals should not be friends with habitual liars or those who do not share a similar set of ethics. Empaths can be persuadable to a fault, making them easy targets for those whose intentions are not so altruistic.

- **Reading the emotions of others:** Empaths can easily read the emotions of other people as well as animals. When standing on the outside of a discussion or debate, empaths hone in on the emotional energies of the parties observed. Whether consciously or otherwise, empaths have the ability to read body language and determine which emotions are really being communicated.

- **Difficulty with indirect communication:** Empaths are notoriously challenged when it comes to understanding subtle cues or "getting" what is being conveyed in an indirect manner. Empaths will often become confused when others are trying to help them get the hint about something, which is why it is so difficult for them to perceive social boundaries unless they are explicitly expressed. Communication that is implied or subversive does not sit well with empaths, as they thrive on direct and honest communication. It takes practice to learn how to read between the lines, but empaths can worry about this less if they choose to communicate primarily with those who speak directly and honestly.

- **Sensitivity to stimuli:** Physical sensations are heightened for empaths. While an average person might smell a rose, a highly empathic person might take the rose's scent to an emotional place, discerning its subtle aroma and the memories it evokes. This sensitivity holds true for smell, taste, touch, hearing, and vision. No wonder empaths can't stand raucous noises and bright fluorescent lighting!

- **An attraction to all things mystical:** Empaths enjoy studying things that the majority of people may not even consider exploring. The cultures, religions, and diverse practices of the world's inhabitants are fascinating and beautiful to them. Empaths desire to step into the experiences of others because it reminds them that we all are not as separate as it may sometimes appear. Even if someone else's practice or culture seems intimidating to some, empaths thirst for the knowledge it can bestow. In this way, life is an experience of understanding and creating cultural and spiritual bonds. This is one reason why many empaths make excellent anthropologists, sociologists, and psychologists. By understanding others, they can better understand themselves.

- **A pleasant demeanor:** Empaths are nice folks—not always, but most of the time. They cannot stand discord and are likely to be in a frazzled state if they engage in conflict. As natural healers, empaths want what's best for everyone around them. They hate to see others suffering, so they will often make life choices that help reduce the suffering of those around them. Because empaths are proponents of world peace, they will often do whatever it takes to make sure the people around them are getting along—or at least agreeing to disagree. They are accustomed to being told by others, even total strangers, that they believe empaths can be trusted with anything.

- **Social anxiety:** During highly social situations, the empath's senses are alight. At these times, they are processing various levels of reality all at the same time. Even the smallest interaction can be seen as carrying psychological, emotional, and spiritual significance. Empaths prefer to receive and process pieces of sensory input at a steady pace rather than receive an overload of stimuli all at once. In social situations this can be tricky and can lead to a pattern of social anxiety or even social phobia if left untreated. We will explore methods of working with social anxiety later in this chapter.

- **A desire for solitude:** Experienced empaths know the value of taking personal time when needed. It is not a good idea to isolate oneself from society for extended periods of time, but it is essential to get some space now and again. When empaths have some time to themselves, they can relax their senses and calm their energies before once again engaging with the world. Even brief moments of solitude can realign the spirit with a greater sense of peace.

- **Feelings of alienation:** In a world in which extreme terror and cruelty are all too common, it's easy to feel like an alien in human form. As empaths observe humanity's mass delusions and social illnesses, a part of them wants to help heal the world, while the other part feels disconnected from civilization entirely. Understandably, they often feel that they are on the outside looking in on a world that doesn't value compassion and unity. Regardless, empaths are here for a reason and should rejoice in the fact that they are different from the norm! It's beautiful to be an alien.

## Labels and Identity

For many sensitive souls, the term *empath* can be both affirming and empowering. We can gain a sense of confidence by knowing that we are different from the norm. Who wants to be normal anyway? We are here to help usher the world into a greater level of compassion, and as long as we can maintain that positivity toward others (and ourselves), we're doing our job in the world. If using the term *empath* invokes a sense of confidence in you, why not use it with pride?

Just remember that being highly empathic is not a reason to avoid personal responsibility and accountability. Your empathic nature is not to blame for everything that goes wrong. Empathy can certainly contribute to times when we feel overwhelmed, but we do ourselves a disservice if we blame all of life's woes on our emotional predisposition. Instead of viewing empathy in this light, try asking yourself how you can utilize your skills as an empath to heal your wounds and replace stress with love.

Labels are categories that many people agree upon, providing a point of reference when information is being transmitted. They can help us easily identify and categorize life on earth. If you don't feel comfortable with a certain term, there is no need to identify with it. Because life is one big spectrum of diversity, it is entirely up to you which identifiers you choose to use.

*We are here to help usher the world into a greater level
of compassion, and as long as we can maintain that
positivity toward others (and ourselves), we're doing
our job in the world. If using the term "empath" invokes
a sense of confidence in you, why not use it with pride?*

⊙

### Compassionate Response

Emotions help us engage with reality. Without emotions, only base survival instincts would exist. Survival perspectives of "fending for oneself" and "me versus them" can be seen as rooted in fear, whereas "happiness for all" and "global compassion" are clearly based in love. Empathy and love coexist in an undeniably spiritual bond. If we wish to "live love," we must activate our empathic skills both for others and for ourselves.

Empathy *on its own* is not necessarily based in love. Empathy is an emotional experience that is often followed by a response of compassion and kindness, but without this loving response, empathy falls short. For example, we might find ourselves becoming angry when we are around another person (or people) who is upset. This is most definitely an empathic experience, but unless it's followed by a response of compassion, the empathy simply exists without much point or purpose.

When a person's empathy is functioning at its highest potential, feelings of limitless love occur without hesitation. It feels good to be generous and help others in their lives. It's empowering to make others feel valued and praised. It's rewarding to create positive change.

## Emotional Contagion

A scientific term that is valuable in understanding the empathic experience is *emotional contagion*. The term *contagion* is linguistically similar to *contagious*, meaning that emotions themselves can be socially contagious. When we "catch" an external emotion, we take it on board in our own emotional body. At this point, it can sometimes be difficult to discern the emotion's origin: *Is it mine or is it someone else's, or is it a combination of the two?*

We often see emotional contagion demonstrated in children. If a child is having a grand ol' time playing in the grass, their playmate is likely to feel the same feeling of elation. If one of them gets hurt and starts crying, it's likely that the other child will begin crying too—they have "caught" their friend's emotion without even thinking about it. Younger children also have far less defined social boundaries than adults, making it easy for them to quickly absorb emotional energy.

When we adults "catch" an emotion, it can sometimes be just as challenging to shake it off. If we actively work on cultivating emotional self-awareness, we can more easily recognize an external emotion and see it for what it is. When we become aware of an emotion, we can choose to work with it in a constructive manner.

------------

*If we actively work on cultivating emotional self-awareness, we can more easily recognize an external emotion and see it for what it is. When we become aware of an emotion, we can choose to work with it in a constructive manner.*

## *The Place of Emotions*

Society is a complicated beast, and for those who are highly empathic, it can feel tempting to disconnect from others when the going gets rough. The truth is that empaths can thrive very well in social situations when they are in a balanced state of mind, body, and spirit. Techniques for ensuring holistic health will be explored later in these pages.

Emotions are here to help guide us in life, not to hinder our development. Social scientists overwhelmingly agree that empathy is directly linked to evolution. Evolution is not focused solely on personal physical survival but is dependent on the survival and adaptation of social groupings as well.

Before beginning my journey into empathic discovery, I had no idea that empathy could actually be an evolutionary trait. For many of my younger years, it felt unnatural and even painful to be someone who could actually *absorb* other people's emotions without even trying. However, those woes were borne of someone who didn't have empathic control. Now that I've developed more skill and awareness in this realm, it's easy to see how a *balanced* level of empathy can be socially constructive.

As social beings, we rely on the emotions of others to gauge our interactions. Emotional awareness, including sympathy and empathy, alerts us to potentially dangerous situations and can help ensure our survival. Emotions increase our "fitness," or adaptability, as a species, deterring us from danger and drawing us toward safety. Just the same, empathy and other emotional abilities allow us to form stronger social and familial bonds. When a society is bonded, the entire group can benefit and survive much more easily. Empathy is a social building block that sidesteps the self in order to make room for the whole, ensuring a greater level of evolutionary success for everyone involved.

### Everyday Empathic Techniques

Emotional challenges exist for empaths on a daily basis, even if they are relatively small occurrences. These challenges can become less and less intense over time if we dedicate ourselves to coming back to center and remembering that we don't always have to be perfect. Life is a learning experience, so all we can do is keep trying our best every day.

Social life can be tedious for empaths, so there are a number of things to keep in mind in daily life. In order to promote healthy emotional functioning, empaths would do well to remember a few things when functioning in day-to-day society, including the following points:

- **We don't need to have all the answers:** Sometimes it's enough to listen to, support, and validate the emotions and perspectives of others. Because empaths are natural healers, we inherently want to help solve people's problems and alleviate their suffering. There are times when this is possible, but sometimes the best thing for us to do is provide emotional support for those who are also learning valuable life lessons at their own pace.

- **It's good to be honest:** Although empaths have a natural inclination to save face by not disappointing others, living authentically as empowered empaths requires that we be honest with ourselves and others. By understanding our own perspectives and beliefs, we can more easily define ourselves for who we really are instead of absorbing whatever may be around us.

- **Disapproval is okay sometimes:** While it may be easier to take other people's perspectives on board, we must first examine whether or not these beliefs hold true for us personally. We have the ability to run our experiences through mental and emotional filters in order to see if we truly resonate with any given perspective. Additionally, it's okay if someone disagrees with us from time to time. We are not required to please everyone at all times. Some degree of social disapproval, discomfort, and disagreement is healthy.

- **You are not a victim:** It's easy to get trapped in a victim mentality. This is not a degrading term and is not a permanent state of being, but it is a mental trap that we are all prone to fall into from time to time. We must gain the courage to transform sorrow (including feeling sorry for oneself) into constructive action. It's not enough to buckle down and let life's challenges take control. No matter the circumstances, we have the ability to process our emotions, heal ourselves, protect ourselves, and make the conscious choice to humbly learn from our experiences. We can choose a path of accepting the past, cultivating forgiveness, and lifting ourselves back up when we fall.

- **Put yourself first:** If we wish to serve others and lift them up emotionally, it is essential that we prioritize our own health and wellness on every level. When we feel imbalanced, the empathic experience can work against us and create more social challenges than solutions. By spending periods of time alone (without totally disengaging!), we can assess and reassess our holistic health and seek to realign ourselves and achieve a healthier and better functioning state of being.

- **Cultivate gratitude:** The fact that you are reading this book at this very moment shows that you are literate and have access to material items beyond mere food and shelter. Compared to people in much of the world, we live in luxury in developed nations. Life is not without its problems of course; some challenges in life can make us feel like we just can't handle the experience of living. At the end of the day, we are very lucky and can create deeper healing in our lives if we remember the gifts and opportunities that we have been given. We must maintain a perspective of the bigger picture in order to thrive both personally and socially as the highly sensitive souls that we are.

## Empathic Brain, Empathic Mind

In many ways, empaths are like social mirrors. We are accustomed to experiencing emotions around us whenever they occur. For some, this happens instantaneously and creates emotional confusion. Empaths who are more developed and skilled in personal techniques tend not to allow external emotions to overwhelm them unless their guard is down. One way to accomplish this is to understand the emotional process cognitively and rationally.

I remember when I quit smoking cigarettes on 11/11/11. In addition to performing spiritual work to help break the addiction, I studied material that promoted a *rational* understanding of the addiction process. Rather than making the reader feel ashamed, the stop-smoking material I studied was empowering because it explained how the addiction works on a physiological and a psychological level. As discussed, the mind, body, and emotions all work together in unison, each affecting the others. By understanding the physical and psychological functioning of cigarette addiction, I was able to separate myself from the desperation of "craving," creating greater health and wellbeing. I should also mention that cigarettes and other addictions actually increase stress and anxiety. Empaths benefit on countless levels by overcoming addiction of any variety.

### Mirror Neurons and Hormones

I see empathy as both a metaphysical and a biological process. Physiologically, a healthy brain is wired to experience empathy to one degree or another, and this is greatly due to neurological processes.

Neurons are part of the nervous system. These cells transmit information by way of synapses in a process called *neurotransmission*. Different neurons have different functions. For example, motor neurons help us move and function by way of nerve signals, while sensory neurons tell us how our body is responding to sensory stimuli. The human brain is host to about 100 billion neurons, with over two hundred of them firing every second—that's a lot of processing power!

Some recent scientific research has given rise to the identification of what are called *mirror neurons* existing within the beautiful squishy organ of the brain. These neurons specialize in creating a cognitively empathic experience in an onlooker. For example, do you ever cross your legs next to someone who is also crossing their legs or clear your throat after hearing someone else clear their throat? I *know* you yawn when you see someone else yawn—maybe the very mention of yawning is creating a yawn right now. (I'm right there with ya.) All these experiences are examples of mirror neurons at work in our brain.

In terms of evolutionary survival, humans and other animals will often mimic others' subtle behaviors in order to understand them, thereby putting them in a better position to predict the other person's behavior. Motor mimicry also allows us to better connect with others by helping us stand in their shoes, so to speak. This identification creates stronger social bonds, aiding in increasing a species' social strength and evolutionary prospects.

It is believed that the *supramarginal gyrus* is the area of the brain most likely responsible for the empathetic experience. This is located in the cerebral cortex near the front of the brain. When someone lacks physiological activity in this region of the brain, they are likely to demonstrate fewer empathic characteristics socially. Additionally, the hormone *oxytocin* is greatly responsible for the experience of empathy. Known as a "love hormone," oxytocin helps transmit pleasurable sensations and is the body's natural antidepressant. Since this hormone aids in bonding and social pleasure, it is only natural for empathy to be encouraged through the release of oxytocin.

## Emotional Cognition

In addition to empathic brain functioning, we must also pay attention to *cognitive* empathic functions. Empathy and mental cognition go hand in hand. Our responses to emotions affect our mental state and whole-body functioning. In order to differentiate between our own emotions and those of others, we must bring the emotion itself into our awareness. It is by observing and examining our emotions from a cognitive place that we can begin to see them for what they are. From here, we can more easily determine their origins and gain a sense of relief when life feels overwhelming.

Processing emotions through a mental filter requires a sort of stepping back. Empaths have a tendency to dive into and become overtaken by emotional stimuli, so we must commence mental filtration at the first signs of emotional stress. If we can catch ourselves before we emotionally spiral, we can more positively and proactively target our emotions from a place of mindfulness.

The next time you feel emotionally overwhelmed, take a little time to *think* about what you are experiencing. Keep in mind that your brain processes an incredible amount of information at any given time, and this cognitive information can be quickly translated into emotion. Remember that emotions are here to help and guide us, not hold us back. Try examining the emotion from a new vantage point. You may wish to meditate or lie on your back while you do this. Hold the challenging or overwhelming emotion in your conscious mind, regardless of its potential source. Try viewing the emotion through a mental filter by seeing it as an external force. (Even if the emotion is entirely internal, unaffected by outside forces, it is still beneficial to "externalize" it in order to see it in a new light.)

As you hold the emotion in your mind's eye, see if it takes any sort of shape or form. Identify it as something that exists outside of you, and begin communicating with it. Speak your healing intentions to the emotion itself. Tell the emotion that you don't want it to overwhelm you at this time. Tell it to help you learn the life lessons it is trying to teach. Examine the emotion and look for its source—however, don't look too closely for it. If the source is not revealed to you quickly, you are likely not meant to know its origin at this time. Remember that your emotions as an empath are often the result of the interplay between "self" and "other," and it does no good to play an emotional blame game with others.

Throughout this process of externalizing and identifying your emotion from a cognitive perspective, please don't tell the emotion to go away. Developmentally, it does no good to banish our emotions; instead, we want to learn from them. Throughout this process you are *telling* your emotion to do certain things. You are not *asking* it to listen to you, because a mere ask is quite passive. If you are not firm, it may not listen. At the same time, you don't want to forcefully command the emotion unless the situation warrants it (such as with a legitimate panic attack). Finally, keep in mind that you are talking to *yourself* and your own subconscious throughout the process. With repeated practice, you can discover what works best for you to mentally process emotional stress.

By understanding how empathy works in the brain, as well as how to mentally process emotional overload, we grow as individuals and can better help others who may be going through similar experiences.

## Metaphysically Speaking

In recent years, *empathy* has become a widespread term in metaphysical communities. Before scientific and psychotherapeutic fields truly developed an understanding of empathy, the experience likely seemed spiritual and mystical ... even supernatural.

Luckily, empathy is very much natural, normal, and healthy. It's essential to mention that while science may have identified many biophysical realities of the empathic experience, these realizations do not negate the spiritual and mystical aspects of empathy.

As many readers undoubtedly agree, life itself is a spiritual experience. Numerous spiritual seekers and global religions affirm that our souls are wearing these "skin suits" for a brief moment in time while we experience the ups and downs of life. We are here to learn and to spiritually evolve to our higher potential, lifetime after lifetime. Empathy is part of this process of growth.

### Emotional Psychicism

Sometimes called *emotional psychics*, those who can be termed empaths experience a consistently high level of empathy throughout their lives. Empaths experience constant emotional stimulation, appearing to feel everything on a deeper level than the majority of society. While we have examined the scientific nuances of the empathic experience, it is undeniable that there is more to empathy than mere biology.

Those who can be termed *psychics* have an enhanced ability to perceive energies that are often out of the normal realm of human awareness. Psychics who demonstrate precognition can often see how the future is likely to unfold. Those who have retrocognition often get impressions of circumstances related to the past and are able to more easily identify the present moment as a result of prior situations. Other psychics demonstrate skills such as mediumship, which is the ability to both perceive and communicate with disembodied spirits such as ghosts and ancestors, while others are more prone to perceive nonhuman entities such as angels, demons, faeries, spiritual guardians, spirit animals, and deities. Other psychics receive intuitions mainly when dreaming, while in deep meditation, or while performing astral projection. Others are stronger in the realm of medical intuition, having the ability to sense imbalances in others' physical bodies. Most psychics experience a combination of these modes of perception, creating a unique psychic experience for each practitioner. It is realistic to say that everyone is psychic to one degree or another, and the same holds true for empathy.

Psychic experiences are related to the cognitive or mental plane, whereas empathy functions from an emotional level of perception. Most people with a high level of psychic or empathic ability tend to be either predominantly psychic or predominantly empathic. Empaths are quick to recognize and "step into" the emotions of others but sometimes lack the intellectual discernment it takes to step back and help from a rational angle. Traditional psychics, on the other hand, may be able to identify emotions but not necessarily work with them in a way that encourages resolution. It is for this reason that empaths must balance their experiences with cognitive awareness and traditional psychics must balance their extrasensory perceptions with empathetic compassion. Again, the mind and emotions work in unison.

### *Spiritually Sharing*

Metaphysically, it is in professions focused on wellness and healing that we see empathy propped up—and understandably so! Psychotherapy itself is a huge proponent of empathy in this day and age, so it's only natural that metaphysical schools of thought value empathy as a profoundly healing force. While we will explore various healing arts later in the book, suffice it to say that empathy permeates any successful healing practice, whether physical or metaphysical or a combination of approaches.

The law of attraction affirms that we co-create our experience of reality with others around us. If we activate empathy in daily life, both for ourselves and for others, we invite deeper levels of compassion into our experience. If we strive to balance ourselves emotionally, we invite that balanced energy into our everyday life. We can choose to channel these intentions into prayers, meditations, spells, visualizations, and other metaphysical approaches, and we can even communicate wholeheartedly with the divine. Most importantly, we can choose to sustain a balanced level of empathy throughout daily life. When we allow for healthy everyday empathy to occur, we attract more empathic experiences and in some way give permission for others to activate their own empathic guiding light.

### Forms of Empathy

When researching metaphysical aspects of empathy, one is likely to discover perspectives that affirm different "types" of empaths. This is the idea that "animal empaths" are able to empathize with animals, "nature empaths" are able to empathize with natural environments, "crystal empaths" can create empathic healing by using gemstones, and so on.

While this is a fun idea to consider, I personally think these empathic categories actually do an injustice to empathy as a whole. In truth, empathy itself implies emotion. This is why we cannot have an "emotional empath" on one hand and a "physical empath" on the other. Empathy *is* an emotional experience!

While the empathic experience itself may be similar across the board, everyone is unique and different in their own way. Therefore, if a person is naturally interested in herbal healing, for example, they may find themselves able to communicate with the energies of certain plants, perhaps even with the spirits they perceive as guarding or embodying the energy of certain plants. Still, this doesn't necessarily make them an "herbal empath" but rather an "empath who is skilled in herbalism."

**Exercise:** *Sitting with the Shadow*

We all have them: those inner voices of pessimism and optimism, an angel on one shoulder and a devil on the other. In fact, global religions throughout time have long attributed spiritual titles to these forces, often seeing them as external forces that affect our inner lives. Everything from angels to demons can be categorized based on these opposing forces that influence our patterns of thought, speech, and action. Regardless of culture, many spiritual people take a meditative journey into their own shadow and light in order to understand the extent to which they are "self" and the extent to which they are "other."

In many ways, the origin of our shadowy and light selves is of little importance. What's most important to know is that they exist in our psyche and that we can choose which frequency to step into at any given time.

In this exercise, you are encouraged to meet an aspect of your shadow. If for any reason you feel like you're not ready for this, that's okay; there's no pressure. For those of us who have endured deeply traumatic experiences throughout life's journey, any type of shadow work is best performed with a professional therapist, psychiatrist, or licensed clinical professional counselor. If, however, you feel like going on a simple journey to meet your shadow, please follow the steps below.

I should also mention that in the scope of shadow work, this meditative journey is quite minimal. Depending on how well you "know" your shadow at this point, this exercise may be very easy for you or it may give rise to difficult emotions. Please be your own judge, take it at your own pace, and choose to meet the shadow on your own terms. After all, you are not defined by your shadow, and you are the one in control.

1. Get comfy in a meditative position and dim the lights. You may wish to light candles or a beautiful all-natural incense. (I recommend incense from India or Japan.) Ensure that you are comfortable enough to relax all of your muscles for the duration of the exercise, even if it means lying down on a plush surface.

2. Anoint your Ajna chakra (third eye or brow chakra) with a sacred powder or oil in order to provide additional energetic protection. Please feel free to get creative here. Personally, I like to use *chandan* paste (sandalwood), *vibhuti* (holy ash), or *kumkum* (vermillion powder) for this purpose. If you do not have these Hindu supplies on hand, feel free to use anything from powdered sage to an essential oil such as lavender or tea tree. Follow your intuition.

3. When you're ready, take a series of deep breaths in through the nose and out of the mouth. Pay attention to your breath and your heartbeat. Allow yourself to slip into a meditative state. Allow your mind to calm down and your body to become fully relaxed. Ensure that you feel comfortable and safe and will not be disturbed.

4. In your mind's eye, envision yourself surrounded by darkness. As you look closer, you can make out small specks of light … stars! You are floating in empty space, surrounded by a silent serenity. Take some time to sit with this comforting feeling of being embraced by the vast expanse of the universe. Allow it to remind you that you are a sacred starchild who was born of cosmic dust and shall one day return to the source.

5. See yourself slowly moving forward in space, then moving faster. As you pick up speed, you notice a structure in

front of you. It appears to be a small building. You slow down as you approach the structure. As you get closer, you stop in front of the structure and notice big swinging doors alongside a neon sign that blinks "Café."

6. After taking a few deep breaths, you make the decision to step through the large doors. When you enter the space, you notice that no one else is present—it's only you! You notice that the café is decorated with gorgeous décor from around the world. The hardwood tables throughout are accented by velvety couches and plush chairs. The smell of sweet coffees and teas invades your senses. You feel at peace, at home.

7. As you seat yourself on one of the chairs or sofas, you mentally order herbal tea for two. These large cups of steaming beverage appear before you effortlessly, one in front of you and the other in front of an adjacent chair. Sip your tea and relax in the present moment. You are expecting a guest.

8. You feel the presence of your guest appearing. This guest does not enter through the swinging doors; instead, it slowly begins to appear before you in the adjacent seat. You recognize that this figure is part of you, something deep within you: your shadow self. You begin to perceive the figure.

9. Take note of how the shadow appears to you. Perhaps it appears as a silhouetted doppelgänger or simply as a shifting blob of matter. Whatever the case, allow your shadow to appear before you. Invite it to join you for tea. This particular aspect of your shadow is connected to your own self-limiting beliefs, to your past. This aspect of

shadow remembers emotional imprints from your past that have led to anxieties and insecurities in the present time. Accept this. Honor this. Know that you are safe.

10. As you sit down for tea with this part of your shadow, you feel a sense of compassion and forgiveness radiating toward it. This shadow is a part of you, but its downfall is that it thrives on experiences from the past. You sense that this shadow feels wounded, scared, sad, angry … You feel compassion toward it.

11. You may wish to engage with your shadow by asking it a series of questions. If this communication does not feel comfortable at this time, it's okay; simply feel present in the space. If you choose to engage the shadow, feel free to gently ask it questions that may give you insight into your emotional wellness. This might include inquiries about its origin: *How old are you? When did you become more pronounced in my life? Which experiences in my life created your presence?*

12. If you receive responses from this aspect of your shadow self, acknowledge these sensations and send them light. Allow a feeling of empathetic compassion to surround this shadow. Tell the shadow that you appreciate the role it has played in your life. It has helped teach you many life lessons. You understand that this shadow has manifested as a way to protect you emotionally.

13. Next, come to terms with this darkness. Inform the shadow that you are thankful for its influence in the past but you are ready, able, and willing to handle your life at the present time. Assure it that you are safe and that you have matured and evolved into adulthood. Tell the shadow that

you are confident and capable, that its energy is respected but it exists in the past. Tell the shadow what year it is and how old you are. Tell it that you are safe and are now choosing to embrace the light of hope.

14. When you feel at peace, smile to the shadow and give it blessings of light with namaste hands. See the shadow fading into the background, and take another sip of tea. Mentally give thanks while the shadow fades away. You now feel called to leave the café, with the knowledge that you are welcome to return at any time.

15. As you gracefully exit the building, you find yourself once again surrounded by spacious cosmic bliss. You see yourself accelerating through space. Finally, you return to your physical body and become aware of your senses. Slowly awaken from your meditative journey by wiggling your fingers and toes and slowly moving your arms and legs. Taking deep breaths, become aware of your physical body and then open your eyes to reenter your sacred space here on earth.

16. As you come to a standing position, conclude by verbally giving thanks for the experience. You now feel more at peace with your shadow and have gained some insight into its role in your past. Celebrate the fact that you have formed a more intimate line of communication with your shadow; allow this knowledge to fill you with a sense of confidence, strength, and trust.

chapter two

# Empathic Energy
# & Social Skills

Everyone on earth is a developing empath, but those of us who live with a high level of empathy on a daily basis can easily forget just how important this gift truly is. Life as an empath can actually be more manageable than it seems at times. When we are experiencing emotional overload, it's easy to forget that we actually have the power to control our emotional energies. During the times when we're feeling good about life, we can much more easily observe the energetic flow in social situations.

Because empathy is primarily a social experience, it's within the social sphere that we should pay particular attention to the energetic dynamics at play. From here, we can more easily direct these energies and take control of our abilities.

## The Ins and Outs of Emotional Energy
Life has a way of taking us sensitive folk on rollercoaster rides even when we are not ready for such big adventures. Sometimes

we feel like sponges who absorb emotions and get all puffed up with more energy than we can handle. This can lead to feelings of depression and emotional overload and a desire to isolate ourselves socially.

There are times in every empath's life when we feel hopelessly overtaken by the emotional energy around us. It's a struggle to learn how to control our interactions with external energies, whether emotional or otherwise. Luckily for us, the experience of empathy is *not* a one-way street. You heard that right: our job is not merely to absorb energies but also to act as *catalysts* for emotional transformation.

As an empath, it's probably easy to observe that you "step into" the emotions of others, but have you ever noticed that your very presence around other people influences *their* mood? This is especially true if you spend time around fellow empaths. Every social interaction is a give-and-take situation. Unless the person with whom you're interacting demonstrates very little empathy in general, odds are that you are also having a marked influence on their emotions without even realizing it!

You can take note of this effect by paying close attention in social situations. The next time you feel a heightened sense of emotion, see how it influences those with whom you are interacting. This is particularly observable when your own emotional state is not baseline, or neutral, but is somewhat heightened, such as when you feel especially happy or sad. Witness how those around you modify their behavior to match your own projected emotional state, perhaps with a change in their tone of voice or general demeanor. This can happen at home, at work, at family gatherings, with friends, or in any public situation. When you look closely, you will see that you are not only being *influenced* emotionally but are actually an *influencer*.

### Absorbing and Projecting

When empathy is the topic of discussion, it is almost always seen as an *absorptive* trait: we pick up emotions and must learn how to process them. In reality, empathy is also *projective* in that we have an emotional effect on those around us as well. Energy in, energy out.

When we are feeling our best, it's only right to share that positivity with others. Sometimes all it takes is a bit of visualization to direct our empathic vibes to others in a positive way, even when we are feeling a bit overwhelmed by the emotions around us. In fact, if we are feeling overwhelmed, we can choose to alter our energetic flow to a more projective and positive one, which can also help us avoid anxiety attacks—which are the result of feeling overtaken by external energies. (In my book *Esoteric Empathy*, I dive deeper into the particulars of absorptive and projective empathy. I encourage you to pick up a copy of this book if you wish to delve deeper into aspects of empathy that I'm unable to fully cover in these pages.)

During times of empathetic overload, it's easy for us to feel like helpless drifters in a whirlpool of vibrations all around us. When we are feeling deflated or introspective, we can often become influenced by everything around us, especially emotional energy, because we are overly—and usually unwittingly—absorbing whatever energy is in our sphere. This is because our defenses are down. When we consciously invoke confidence and allow our inner light to shine as positively as possible, we actually turn around this energetic flow. It is a mighty spiral dance to absorb, assimilate, and project energies around us simultaneously. It is during these times when we are at our best as empaths.

In many metaphysical systems of thought, it is believed that the left side of the body is absorptive and feminine and the right side of the body is projective and masculine. Regardless of whether we are left-handed or right-handed, it seems that external energies can enter the left side of the body, while energies that we personally set forth come from the right.

When you find yourself in a social situation, take note of how external energies enter the left side of your body. If these energies are not processed and directed, they will simply sit inside you and brew. By consciously shifting these energies to the right side of your body, you can redirect the flow of energetic traffic toward something more balanced.

### Emotional Transmutation

The really neat thing about having a high level of empathy is that we can take this energy exchange one step further. Because we absorb energy so easily and have the option of projecting it, the most crucial factor is how we process the energy before redirecting it. When energy enters our body—and this doesn't have to be just social energy; it can also be energy based in nature or the cosmos—that energy sits within us for a time, even if for only an instant.

When external energy enters our body, we have the option of *transmuting* or *transforming* it into other things. Again, we must feel confident and secure in ourselves in order to do this in a constructive way. By allowing the energy to sit within us briefly, we can take the energy and actually *raise its vibration* into something even more beneficial!

Please note that in instances of anger or aggression, you may visualize the external energy as fiery red, orange, or yellow. During these times, you should visualize this energy instantly settling down within you and transforming into watery and compassionate vibrations. The process of transmuting negative energy into positive energy is challenging, but it *is* possible and is very important to experiment with in daily life.

This whole process of absorption, transmutation, and projection happens very quickly, usually without us realizing it. Emotional absorption can occur when we're on the phone, watching TV, reading the newspaper, or in other everyday scenarios that affect our emotions. Emotional energy is everywhere.

In the case of solitary absorption of energy, such as with the TV or the news, experiment with projective empathy in different ways. Try visualizing blue or white energy projecting from your right hand or the right side of your body. If you are trained in Reiki or other energetic arts, utilize these skills to project your empathic transmutations, or simply do what feels natural.

For example, if you learn of something terrible and unjust occurring in the world, do not give in to these lower energies related to fear. It is all too easy to absorb the fears and sorrows of victims (whether human, animal, or environmental) and allow them to overtake your emotions. This is not a healthy or productive response, even if you can empathize with the feeling of victimhood.

Instead, in such an instance, begin by acknowledging the terror: accept that it exists. Next, hold that energy in your heart center and see the sorrow transforming into hope. Once you legitimately feel confident enough to send hope to the victims in whatever scenario you've encountered—which truly *is* part of your responsibility as an empath—use your skills of energetic projection to *send* this transformed emotion to them through time and space. In most cases of empathic transmutation, the focus is on transforming a frequency of fear into a frequency of love: love for others we encounter along life's journey as well as for ourselves.

There is no need to be in close proximity to the party to whom you are sending a dose of transformed emotional energy. Numerous spiritual systems understand that an invisible, multidimensional web connects everything in the world. It's not only traditional psychics and mystics who can access this network; empaths can quite easily tap into the world's grid of emotional energy as well. (This is also why we empaths find our emotions so affected during times of global catastrophes and natural disasters.)

Just the same, if you encounter something very *positive* and uplifting in the news or in a documentary or what have you, allow that positive flow to continue and even amplify through your own energetic field. Yessiree, you can actually boost these good vibes and help perpetuate them throughout the world!

As an empath, your projections create an emotional ripple effect, which is why we should always be responsible and accountable for our own energetic state. This is why we must keep ourselves balanced and healthy in life to the best of our ability.

Please see the exercise at the end of this chapter to learn a practical everyday method for harnessing and transmuting empathic energy for the greater good.

————————

*There is no need to be in close proximity to the party to whom you are sending a dose of transformed emotional energy. Numerous spiritual systems understand that an invisible, multidimensional web connects everything in*

*the world. It's not only traditional psychics and mystics
who can access this network; empaths can quite easily
tap into the world's grid of emotional energy as well.*

# Everyday Interactions

I can't count the number of times I've heard people tell me that their empathic abilities feel like a curse. Aah! No! Quite the contrary: we are meant to help the world enter a new eon of compassion, health, unity, and (of course) empathy.

But I understand this feeling of dread. Because we empaths are so open to the emotions around us and we feel things so deeply ourselves, we can feel alienated or even freakish. When we learn techniques to positively direct emotional energy for ourselves and others, we can more easily conquer our fears and challenges.

### *Shutting Down and Isolating*

It is important to mention that there is no way to shut off our empathic abilities. Although fears and traumatic imprints might be begging us for emotional anesthetization, this fearful response lacks love and compassion, primarily for ourselves.

Some empaths try to change themselves because empathy feels altogether too burdensome. Some sensitive souls turn to drug abuse, alcoholism, prolonged video gaming, and other methods of emotional disassociation in order to cope. Luckily, many empaths I've spoken with who have fallen into these traps have made the steadfast decision to seek help from professionals, accept healing, and lift themselves back up.

Short periods of social disconnection and isolation can do wonders for empaths, but prolonged periods can create a dependence on being reclusive as a method of emotional self-preservation. As is the case with other potential addictions, most people can function in a healthy way with a little alcohol, a little cannabis, a little video gaming, or a little social distancing. Overindulging in these things, however, can be emotionally damaging.

During tedious times, our first instinct may be to isolate ourselves from others in order to avoid further pain. This is a form of instinctive self-protection. Although this response might feel comforting, it neglects the other individuals in the equation by limiting the potential for a timely resolution to the real issue. When we shut people out, we are left to our own devices. The mind and its insecurities can play dreadful tricks on our conscious beliefs about others and ourselves. Stressful times may require brief periods of "taking space," but this reaction in excess can cause more damage. When we bravely seek social resolution, we open the door to increased self-awareness and are given the opportunity to learn important life lessons.

If we isolate ourselves from society for prolonged periods of time, we are left with our mind alone, processing external stimuli from the internet, books, magazines, television, and so on. During these energetic interactions, we become more prone to absorbing external energies and not accurately projecting our own positive influence. Social isolation can lead to pessimism, bitterness, and even apathy.

Instead of attempting to mute our empathic abilities altogether, we deserve to find healing in whatever form it takes. For ideas on how to work with destructive empathetic thinking, please see chapter 5.

A number of years ago, I discovered a significant reason for my emotional pessimism and social anxiety. Although others around me were saying that I was too concerned with what other people thought about me—and certainly this desire for constant approval is a widespread issue—I came to find out that my own *seriousness* was socially damaging. I was creating a lot of anxiety for myself by taking everything in life too seriously.

Since then, I have been able to combat this tendency by willfully becoming a goofball or a joker at times. I consciously choose to laugh out loud if my spirit wants to. I often make the decision to lift people out of their own seriousness by injecting some positive humor into the situation. Noble efforts such as these may take some time and effort to become routine, but they can go a long way toward combating social anxiety, and they can lead to an increase in overall health and empathic wellness.

---

*Some empaths try to change themselves because empathy feels altogether too burdensome. Some sensitive souls turn to drug abuse, alcoholism, prolonged video gaming, and other methods of emotional disassociation in order to cope. Luckily, many empaths I've spoken with who have fallen into these traps have made the steadfast decision to seek help from professionals, accept healing, and lift themselves back up.*

### Everyday Empathic Techniques

Here are some techniques we empaths can use to better manage our empathy on a daily basis, both socially and independently. These are a few methods that work for myself and other empaths I've consulted with. Everyone has their own unique way of managing emotional energy, so please feel free to modify and add to these techniques and discover what works best for you.

- **Eye contact:** When you're feeling overwhelmed in a conversation, shift your eye contact to the other person's third eye chakra (Ajna) instead of looking directly into their eyes. A huge amount of energy and information is projected through the eyes, so disconnecting momentarily from direct eye contact can prevent an overload of information from entering your own consciousness. You can try this with a fellow empath first. Even they will admit that they can't tell you are looking at their brow instead of their eyes!

- **Headwear:** If you must have social interactions during a time when you feel especially introverted, experiment with wearing a hat or other type of headgear. Whether you're wearing a hat, wig, bandanna, veil, or anything else on your head, you're likely to discover that covering your crown chakra (Sahasrara) can have a grounding effect by bringing your energy back down into your body and can help create clearer communication. Just be sure not to get too dependent on covering yourself in public; if it becomes a crutch, the beneficial effects it has will fade.

- **Confidence:** The good ol' axiom "Fake it till you make it" comes into play here. During those times when you feel particularly deflated, introverted, or melancholy, try shifting your body language to communicate "confidence" to your brain. Pull back your shoulders, look straight ahead, walk upright, don a smile, and communicate clearly. It's not that you're being fake, but you are in fact amplifying your positive qualities by slightly exaggerating these traits. Although this may feel counterintuitive and even disingenuous at first, you will soon get into a pattern of invoking true confidence when it's needed most. When you do this, make an effort *not* to attach your ego to this confidence; your confidence should be along the lines of inner strength, capability, and self-assuredness rather than some sort of feigned arrogance.

- **Insta-grounding:** Everyone has a different way of grounding and centering themselves. Some people carry a rock or gemstone, while others practice *pranayama*, or breathing exercises. There are innumerable *healthy* ways you can return to center and ground back into your body. Use your intuition to discover methods to accomplish this throughout daily life, and modify these practices to suit your needs when you're in a public setting versus when you're on your own.

- **Recognize your comrades:** There is a time in every empath's life when we lose sight of our own social wellbeing, often due to a perceived need to please everyone around us. But boundaries are okay, limitations are a virtue, and being selective is a healthy practice. If you feel like you are surrounding yourself with nonprogressive individuals who appear to *take* compassion more than they offer it up, take note and modify your social interactions. While this might be challenging to do in a workplace or at an academic institution, for example, your personal time is extremely valuable. You deserve to be surrounded by fellow compassionate souls as well as people who constructively challenge you, rather than those who unwittingly create a burden of stress or shame. Your spiritual comrades should be guiding lights along life's journey, just as you are for them.

## Communication Skills

Discovering comfortable modes of communication can be a life-long journey for empaths. For starters, we have the challenge of getting *lost in emotion* during conversation, sometimes losing track of what is being said with words. This hyper focus on emotional communication over verbal communication can actually lead to increased anxiety, especially if your conversational partner surmises that you are not paying attention to them. When this happens, you are likely to feel ashamed because you upset your partner in conversation. If this happens to you, try telling the person verbally that you, as a highly empathic person, were sensing their emotions but were still paying attention, then shift yourself to a predominantly mental or cognitive focus. Try to summarize some of what they said to you in order to make sure that you understood their communication accurately. A little humility is a good thing, but humiliation is not! Look your conversational partner in the eye, nod your head when you need to, and pay attention to the manner in which they are communicating. We can use our empathy to shift our awareness to another person's method of communication instead of simply getting lost in their emotional fluctuations.

It's easy to get lost in emotions in social situations, so it's both wise and courageous to hone the ability to shift between emotional and mental communication with others. Let's explore a few tips to keep in mind when human communication is necessary.

### Prioritizing Others

We empaths can massively overthink our experiences, even when the situation doesn't really warrant such obsessive behavior.

Much of the time, this overthinking is directed at ourselves. After all, we are our own worst critics.

It's essential to know that we get to choose our emotional responses. This can be easier said than done, but with enough practice we can proactively choose to disallow depressive, isolating, or self-deprecating thoughts from overtaking our heart space.

The act of prioritizing other people throughout daily life is a powerful remedy to combat a self-defeating tendency. We don't need to take everything in life personally, because sometimes it's just not about us. Exercising care for others requires us to second-guess our own insecurities and self-limiting beliefs on a regular, consistent basis.

Highly empathic people genuinely care about others—it's in our nature! When we find ourselves turning inward to an unhealthy degree, we can respond by taking a deep breath and affirming, "I'm okay. I can handle this."

Naturally, we empaths must tend to our own emotional garden first and foremost. Incidentally, we can actually cultivate personal emotional healing simply by putting others first—as long as we know that we ourselves are healthy and safe. The act of prioritizing others' emotional, mental, and physical safety can do wonders for our own emotional wellness.

It takes a good dose of humility to take on the role of peacemaker, mediator, or caregiver when we aren't feeling at our best. Just remember: we don't have to solve everybody's problems. Sometimes it really is enough to provide support by offering a shoulder to lean on, a listening ear, or a trustworthy connection.

## *Discerning Communication Cycles*

Before we can learn to have accurate and bonding communication with others, we must consciously examine the communication we have with ourselves. Because empaths are naturally sensitive, it's far too easy for us to read into every little thing. This can lead to a cycle of drama that neither we nor anyone else in our life actually deserves to deal with! Sure, it's essential to communicate concerns, insecurities, and negative thoughts that run through our overthinking mind, but sometimes our mind plays tricks, so we can't always take our own thoughts at face value.

The world is not against us. In fact, many would say that our daily experiences, including all of the challenges, are karmically aligned. We experience joys and hardships in life that help refine us as individuals. We are often presented with similar cycles of experience until we are able to humbly learn the life lessons that are held within the repeating challenge.

These patterns of relationship can occur with friends, lovers, colleagues, family, and even those with whom we seldom interact. We may find ourselves experiencing the same type of challenge over and over with different individuals in our life. When we begin to recognize our own reactive patterns—and the cyclical experiences that the universe seems to be delivering—we can break the cycle with humility and acceptance. But first we must distinguish between fact and fiction in our communications.

Cyclical challenges are so often rooted in communication, both with others and within ourselves. Internally, we are constantly faced with the challenge of interpretation. If someone says, "Hey, I like your hairstyle," we might choose to accept the compliment and allow it to boost our confidence, even for just a moment. On the other hand, we might choose to view the statement as being loaded or disingenuous. We might interpret the comment as "they are actually just making fun of me" or "that means my hair looked awful last week." Indeed, it's our choice whether or not to twist something in our mind into something that may or may not exist. And while it's true that passive-aggressive communication is far too common in society, it's ultimately up to us to determine whether or not we really need to be reading between the lines.

When we consciously choose positive thinking—even if it feels counterintuitive at first—we find ourselves less affected by criticism. By thinking positively, we choose to maintain a healthier self-image, which in turn disallows negative mental patterns from overtaking us. The choice of optimism is especially vital if we have a tendency to believe the worst possible things about any given social exchange.

The mind is not the enemy; in fact, it can be our best friend. When we get to know how our mind works, including any pessimistic patterning, our consciousness can actively differentiate between fact and fiction. From there, our emotions can enter a more balanced state of being.

There's no sense in replaying the same self-destructive worries over and over in our heads. Admittedly, I have a longtime pattern of doing this. However, I'm getting better at recognizing this mental pattern on a day-to-day basis, and I encourage you to try to do the same.

One thing I've noticed is that I'm prone to obsess about difficult social experiences and self-limiting beliefs because my mind wants to problem-solve. There is a positive side to this in that it involves a willingness to put things on the table instead of emotionally repressing them, but there's a fine line. If the other person and I are not able to come up with a solution in the here and now, there's no sense in getting worked up about something that can't be immediately remedied. Obsession can cloud the mind, convincing us of numerous horrors that are actually far from reality. If we can instead respond with patience and trust, we will be more equipped to problem-solve when time allows.

### Engaging Socially

When we're in a good mood, we're more apt to engage socially in a positive, healthy, uplifting manner. This becomes possible when we choose to see the good in any situation instead of expecting the worst. Life is full of ups and downs, especially for highly empathic souls, but it does no good to set ourselves up for social failure simply because we've gotten burned in the past.

Painful social experiences can create imprints, whether conscious or subconscious, that can make us prone to negative *expectations*. We might feel as though we are being judged constantly. We might allow ourselves to flip out over the smallest occurrences or internally fixate on irrational fears. When we expect the worst, we often create a self-fulfilling prophecy. In other words, our thoughts and expectations can actually play a part in creating, or *re*-creating, negative experiences in our lives. When we confirm our darkest thoughts, we may feel some sort of internal justification, but this habitual pattern does not actually empower or engage us socially; it only fosters depression.

Instead of holding on to negative social experiences from the past, allow yourself to think about the amazing positive social exchanges you've also enjoyed. Without a doubt, your positive interactions far outweigh the negative ones, even though the negative experiences feel heavier. Simply shift your focus.

When it comes to engaging socially, remember that the vast majority of interpersonal communication comes from body language and vocal tone. This is why emails and texts are so impersonal, not to mention dreadfully easy to misconstrue. When communicating in person, try bringing mindful awareness to the body language and vocal tone of both yourself and the other party. Notice the empathetic exchange that occurs between you and the other person as a result of these factors. Notice your posture, facial expressions, eye contact, and nervous tics. Observe how your vocal tone affects the whole conversation, and decide whether or not you are projecting an empathically constructive or destructive energy beyond the mere words being spoken.

Self-awareness during communication can be difficult to achieve because there are so many factors at play. Communication occurs on multiple levels all at once. We are social creatures by nature. When the ins and outs of communication seem overwhelming, keep in mind that it's a process. We don't have to be perfect, and we can learn from our mistakes. Also, rest assured that you have been communicating with others all your life, so it's simply a matter of adaptation. Adaptation is evolution.

When a person cannot gauge our emotional state accurately or read our social cues, they are likely to see us as "dangerous" on a subconscious level. This is animal instinct. When we feel like we can read or understand a person, it creates a level of safety. When we know where another person is at, we can make informed decisions about them based on the level of comfort we feel. The more comfort and trust there is, the more vulnerable and honest we can choose to be. This is why relationships of any type take work, dedication, and a two-way focus on total honesty.

Along similar lines, we must strive to be dependable. This doesn't just mean getting to work on time but relates to the consistency of our everyday actions. Social wellness relies greatly on dependability, because then others know what to expect. When we behave with emotional consistency, we can be seen as reliable and trustworthy, even despite any emotional shortcomings. Social rapport is built on trust, and trust is built on dependability.

Empowered social engagement occurs when we feel confident in our empathic abilities. By bringing acute self-awareness to our own methods of communication, we can instantly shift the energy of an exchange from one of total emotional absorption to something more reciprocal.

### *Exercise:* *Absorptive and Projective Empathy*

As we have explored in this chapter, empathy is not merely the ability to absorb and "become" emotions from external sources. No, no, no—this is a terribly self-limiting belief! A healthy empathic experience is one of emotional reciprocity, not a one-way street of emotional victimization.

In order to free ourselves from these perceived limitations, it's essential that we take a step back and monitor the flow of emotions in our daily life. More often than not, emotional exchanges between ourselves and others occur very quickly, so it can be a challenge to notice and accurately gauge their effects in the moment. Plus, we are so *accustomed* to communicating that we take for granted all the different levels of communication that occur simultaneously in everyday life.

A great step toward accomplishing everyday wellness as an empath is to become aware of the in-flow and out-flow of emotional energy. Because emotions and thoughts are intricately connected, even the mere knowledge of this occurrence is enough to help shift external emotional energy out of our body and into the surrounding environment. What's more, we can actually transform the emotions we have absorbed into something greatly beneficial for ourselves and others. All it takes is a bit of practice and patience.

1. The next time you find yourself in a social situation involving communication between you and another person, bring to mind the energetic flow of the person with whom you are interacting, especially the emotions you sense them feeling. During the process of communication, casually visualize the other person's emotional energy entering your own sphere in your left shoulder area; from here, it can be assimilated with your own energy and harnessed as you see fit.

2. Pay special attention to how these energies instantaneously enter your body in conversation. Take note of how quickly you project your own energy to communicate and add to the discussion at hand. Notice how quickly this process happens. Simply observe these dynamics without getting too sidetracked. The conversation you're having is the most important thing.

3. While observing this process, take note of how much external energy you keep held within your own body: in your chakras, in your aura, in your energetic field—call it what you will. Are you contributing equally to the conversation at hand? Are you fully engaged? Are you giving as much as you are getting? How much external energy in this social

interaction are you keeping held within your own body and energy centers?

4. Next, when emotional energy enters your body during a conversation, visualize it in a blue color. Blue is a color related to the element of water, which is said to rule empathy and intuition. See this blue emotional energy swirling within you; you will sense where it "settles" in your body. In empaths, it is believed that this energy usually sits within the solar plexus chakra (Manipura) or the heart chakra (Anahata).

5. When external emotional energy settles within your body, see it *swirling* around your heart or solar plexus. All energy is movement; nothing in life is stagnant. If you are having a relatively pleasant conversation with another person, simply allow their energy to be absorbed into your body on your left side while they communicate and projected out the right side of your body while you communicate in return. If you wish, you can "add" a dose of white light to this energy by nonchalantly visualizing the energy gaining a boost of light from your heart center. Your heart is the halfway point between the absorption of their energy and the projection of your own. This sounds like a lot of work, but it actually happens quite naturally. In fact, you don't have to shift your focus away from the conversation; instead, this process should allow you to be more fully interactive in the present moment.

6. As you project your own energy out the right side of your body in conversation, envision it entering the other person's sphere. (It is their own decision whether or not to take the energy into their body and reciprocate with conversation.) You may notice their energy entering your body and your

own energy exiting yours at the same time. Remember to visualize a little white light being added to the emotional energy you project in their direction; this is related to the process of emotional transmutation. Again, this process happens very quickly and is a natural part of human communication.

7. During this process of energetic redirection, you will find that these energies follow your words and mannerisms because these actions are themselves projective: they come from you. As you intentionally add a boost of white light to the emotional energies you are projecting, remember that these energies help create your words, and your words help create these energies. As a strong empath, you are a conduit for emotional energy at all times. You are meant to add your own unique dose of positivity and love to this world, one interaction at a time. By practicing this easy visualization in everyday conversation, you may find yourself paying better attention to conversational exchanges, and you may discover that your intentional boost of light helps any given conversation remain positive, optimistic, and lighthearted.

chapter three

# Protection & Discretion

We empaths are no strangers to emotional confusion. Perhaps the most common conundrum we face is not knowing where our own energies end and someone else's begin. It's common for empaths to engage in one-on-one conversations and get lost in the interplay of emotional energies. In most cases, we can easily understand where the other party is coming from and can relate to what they are expressing. Emotionally, we are pickin' up what they are puttin' down, but we have to exercise caution lest we lose ourselves in the other person's perspectives while setting aside our own.

## Mine vs. Yours

Positive interactions with others are a balanced exchange of mental, emotional, and sometimes physical input. When these interactions become predominantly one-sided, we allow the other person or party to become dominant. At times this is beneficial, especially if we don't feel particularly social. If this becomes habitual, however, we open ourselves to the possibility of becoming led or even controlled or manipulated. It is vitally important that we maintain our boundaries, which can be accomplished in a number of ways.

We empaths do not only absorb everyone else's emotions; we ourselves are deeply sensitive souls. The interplay of internal and external emotions can cause a flurry of emotional reactions when it feels beyond our control.

Let's be honest: empaths can be oblivious when it comes to boundaries. More specifically, we often struggle not only with setting our own boundaries but also with sensing and recognizing the boundaries of others. In terms of the latter, I believe this is a manifestation of our empathic ability to recognize and link to emotional energies, which at times causes us to lose track of the intellectual content of the conversation, including subtle cues that indicate social boundaries. Sometimes we just don't get the hint—but hopefully our friends and family will be sympathetic to our plight!

---

*Positive interactions with others are a balanced exchange of mental, emotional, and sometimes physical input. When these interactions become predominantly one-sided, we allow the other person or party to become dominant. At times this is beneficial, especially if we don't feel particularly social. If this becomes habitual, however, we open ourselves to the possibility of becoming led or even controlled or manipulated.*

*Everyday Empathic Techniques*

Here are some tips and tricks for empaths looking to keep external emotional energies separate from their own. Many of these tips apply to social situations, while others focus on solitary energetic work.

1. **Mindfulness:** Mindfulness is a psychological and spiritual process that Buddhism and many other spiritual paths strongly promote. Although it's sometimes easier said than done, it is possible for deep thinkers and deep feelers to take a step back by invoking present-moment awareness. One of my favorite techniques for doing this involves becoming cognitively aware of what is occurring at any given moment. (This ties back into the concept of bringing emotional awareness to the mental plane.) For example, when I am driving in my car and feeling stressed or overwhelmed by a long list of time-consuming errands, I often choose to practice intentional mindfulness. I will start repeating words of perceptive awareness in my head, such as "I am driving, driving, driving…," followed by "I am breathing, breathing, breathing…," followed by specifics, such as "green light…car in front of me…car to my left…red light…slowing down…observing traffic…breathing…," and other similar terms that immediately bring my cognitive attention to what's occurring in the present moment. This allows me to step back emotionally and observe present-moment reality.

2. **Breath and light:** At the time of this writing, I have had numerous social interactions of late with individuals in emotional distress. In times past, my unrestrained empathy would have ensured that I would absorb the emotion, reflect

the emotion, and do nothing but add to the stressful situation. The practice I recommend instead—which requires a healthy amount of self-confidence—is to remember that empaths are meant to help transform and transmute emotional energies, not merely become overwhelmed by their presence. During encounters with distressed individuals, I choose to follow these steps instead. First, I become aware that I am in this situation, surrounded by someone in an emotionally distraught or stressed state. Next, I offer comfort and reassurance in an effort to provide much-needed *support* and to avoid absorbing the emotion. From there, I take a short breath, visualizing myself breathing in the stressful emotion partially into my own body. A quick exhalation follows this, where I swiftly visualize the emotion dispersing and dissolving, with *light* in its place. It's a good idea to follow this visualization with a burst of light, envisioning the energy surrounding, soothing, and supporting the distressed individual. I like to visualize a soothing light quickly descending from the cosmos above, washing over the other person (or both of us), and then gently making its way into the earth below. The efficacy of this technique astounds me, so I hope you will consider practicing it.

3. **Rewind the mind:** We don't always know the source of any particular emotion that overtakes us. Sometimes it's our own, sometimes it's other people's, sometimes it's a combination of the two, and sometimes it's hard to say. During times of emotional overload, it's a wise idea to take a few moments to ground yourself, meditate, and reflect on the day's activities, including the activity of your dreams. Think back to what you experienced over the last twenty-four

hours. Consider the emotional state of others you have been around. This includes the emotional state of anyone in the media you've consumed, such as the television shows or films you've watched or even your online interactions. When recalling the last twenty-four hours, try to recall if you experienced any situation in which the difficult emotions you are experiencing now were present. Could you have empathically absorbed emotional energy from an outside source? Could this energy have influenced your own emotional state? Could this be entirely internal, with your own life's circumstances creating emotional confusion? From this vantage point, you will be better able to constructively *problem-solve* by considering a variety of emotional angles.

4. **Self-identity:** Here is something that empathic folks often forget in the midst of interacting with others: we have our own identities, opinions, and perspectives that are unique and individualistic. At times it may feel as though we are at the whim of whatever emotional energy surrounds us, including emotionally driven perspectives and opinions, but the truth is that we have the ability to formulate our own opinions, viewpoints, and beliefs. When we allow ourselves to simply absorb other people's realities, we do ourselves (and others) a disservice by muzzling our own unique voice in the world. The tendency to absorb and reflect other people's opinions is usually borne of insecurity and a desire to avoid rocking the boat in social settings. It feels good to get along with everyone, but real progress is made in life when we allow ourselves to shine, and sometimes this means having a different opinion. So the next time you find

yourself being a "yes man" in a social situation, try reminding yourself that empathy is not just absorptive but can also be projective. Consider your own personal viewpoints when having discussions with others: bring your mind back to your own identity and make the courageous choice to disagree at times. Although we are all one, we are simultaneously unique, each of us a valuable piece of life's great puzzle.

5. **Eye contact:** One of my earliest empathic realizations was the importance of eye contact. The eyes often can communicate more information than words alone. Do you ever look at a house cat and exchange "slow blinks"? In cat language, these kitty kisses communicate a sense of comfort and safety. Eye contact among members of every animal species is of great significance; even the slightest eye movement can convey a wealth of information. Try applying this knowledge to your own social situations, remembering that eye contact (or the lack thereof) communicates a massive amount of information, both consciously and subconsciously. Become aware of how often you tend to look into the other person's eyes when communicating. Because emotional information is conveyed through eye contact, some empaths shut themselves off from this form of interaction, even if it creates social awkwardness. This is rooted in fear and is not a healthy response in the vast majority of cases. If you find yourself frequently avoiding eye contact, consider that this may be an instinctive method of shielding yourself against a potentially overwhelming emotional exchange. Normal and healthy human communication consists of about 60–70 percent eye contact and 30–40

percent noncontact, such as when you're thinking about something or formulating a response. Take note of ways that you could improve your eye contact skills, and think about the messages you could be conveying in conversation when you engage in or avoid eye contact in any given situation.

6. **Obscuring the brow:** Many mystical systems recognize the crown of the head and the brow as being the areas of the body that are the most open to external energies. Perhaps you have noticed that when a person wears a hat or sunglasses or covers their forehead with their hair, communication with them seems to be somehow different. This is because their upper energy centers (and/or their eyes) are closed off from full engagement. Although it is not advisable most of the time, obscuring the brow can go a long way in keeping our energies to ourselves. I recommend covering these parts of the body in public only when you feel especially vulnerable or are having a bad day. When this method is overused, it can create unwanted social distance by making others feel unengaged, even if it's only subconscious.

7. **Mnemonics:** We are in charge of keeping ourselves emotionally in check every day, as much as possible. We need to maintain a steady level of self-awareness. In fact, some empaths I know even have a "mindfulness bell" app on their phone that dings at regular intervals as a reminder to become self-aware in the moment. I like to remind myself to do this by keeping a mnemonic reminder on my person. For example, if I've been feeling especially ungrounded for whatever reason, I will sometimes carry a polished piece of hematite in both of my pants pockets. Whenever I dig in

my pockets or feel the stones throughout the day, it serves as a reminder to become aware of my personal energy and perform a bit of insta-grounding, such as taking a deep breath or quickly visualizing my shields reinforced (which we'll talk about next). Sometimes I even set an alarm on my phone to remind myself to become self-aware at a particular moment. Mnemonic reminders such as these can help remind us to return to center, take a breath, and calm our energies.

## Shielding and Visualization

It probably goes without saying that empaths, highly sensitive individuals, and a variety of psychics are greatly in need of energetic protection on a regular basis. It's tough work being *this* receptive and open; we need to keep our own energy strong and disallow external influences from overtaking us. We enter dangerous psychological territory when our own energies are pushed aside and replaced with something that's not our own. In fact, some cultures would call this a form of possession. Indeed, we are responsible for being our own advocates *and* our own exorcists!

We need to protect ourselves emotionally and energetically; this is a reality that highly empathic people must face on a daily basis. As discussed earlier, it's deeply important for empaths to maintain a strong sense of identity when interacting socially. Keep in mind that, as with all things, there is a fine balance, and sometimes it takes a bit of trial and error to discover ideal modes of operation. I remember a time in my life when I realized I was allowing everybody else's opinions to shape my personality. In order to please them socially, I would adopt their opinions, whether they were opinions about myself or others or outlooks on life in general. At that time in my life, if my peers felt a certain way about politics, religion, or other people, I would take on those opinions because it felt easier to publicly agree; moreover, this practice allowed me to feel like I was *pleasing* the other person, which served to increase my likability and create a protective feeling of social camaraderie.

After a while, I realized that I had this unhealthy tendency and decided to drastically reverse my behavior. Instead of agreeing all the time, I instead became more defensive and combative. I frequently touted my own differing viewpoints as "facts" in an effort to protect myself emotionally. This projective emotional and intellectual influence started to create a social barrier that was, admittedly, unfair and inconsiderate toward others in my life. Perhaps this reaction is something you can relate to. If not, please consider this a word to the wise so that you can avoid swinging on the same socially disturbing pendulum! Over time, I learned to balance my social interactions so that they became mindful and respectful toward both others and myself.

In addition to some of the advice offered in the previous section, a good technique for instant social protection is to use an internal mental filter rather than respond reactively. While it's good to affirm positive conversations by regularly saying "yeah" and nodding your head, it's actually healthier and more fulfilling to balance this with statements of consideration. In other words, it's more respectful to "sit with" what another person is saying than to only respond affirmatively.

When having conversations, be sure not only to feel the other individual's emotions but also to cognitively process what they are communicating. Really listen to them before mentally formulating responses. When you feel confident, you will find yourself incorporating more instances of saying "hmm," "okay," and "right," for example. When a person feels as though you are mentally processing information and coming to *your own* conclusions, the conversation becomes more genuinely interactive. In addition, by incorporating more cognitive social processing such as this, your own emotional energy naturally becomes more protected as a result of interacting on levels that are not restricted to the emotional sphere.

### Protective Energetics

Empaths can construct shields that act as extensions of their own energy. Shielding is a give-and-take because the barriers depend on our mind and emotions. When we confidently construct shields and hold steadfast to our visualization techniques, our energetic extensions are psychologically strengthened. When we doubt ourselves, question ourselves, or rely on the all-too-easy "I can't" mentality, our shields will be ineffective and virtually nonexistent.

Looking at common beliefs concerning the etheric body, it is widely understood that an invisible field of energy surrounds everything in existence. It is generally assumed that if something is animate, or conscious, it will have a stronger aura due to the complexity of the organism. Because of humankind's unique psychological and emotional constitution, it stands to reason that human auras are especially pronounced and significant. Individuals who work with auras and other nonvisible levels of energy agree that the aura is constantly changing size, shape, and color, depending on a person's mental, emotional, or physical state in any given moment. Intentional energetic shielding, then, is a type of visualization that both protects the aura and works in tandem with our preexisting energy field.

When we intentionally create shields of protection, our mental and emotional states can easily alter and mold the shields. With repeated practice, our shields can take on a life of their own in a sense, becoming more independently existent on the astral plane. By reinforcing something external—even if it originates internally—a type of separation occurs. (If we were to apply this belief of intentional manifestation to religion, magick, and mysticism, it would open a can of worms that these pages could not possibly contain, so let's save that for another time!)

Interactive methods of social shielding can be discovered with practice. Be sure not to place too much pressure on yourself right away; sometimes these things take time. By reflecting on our daily social exchanges, we can learn to fine-tune our interactions and discover what works best for us. Like everyone else, we deserve to feel a sense of emotional safety and security throughout our human experience.

So why am I placing so much emphasis on our everyday social interactions instead of jumping right in to methods of energy protection? The reason for this cannot be stated strongly enough. Although empathic shielding and visualizations are extremely important, the truth is that empaths often have difficulty maintaining these energetic barriers. This is why an empath's most effective techniques of protection can take place during everyday social interactions.

Intentionally practicing shielding with regular visualization is an extremely beneficial practice for sensitive souls of all types. However, unlike with individuals who are not quite as emotionally sensitive, empaths' shields can crumble very quickly in challenging social situations. Whereas someone who is less empathic can more easily default to the shield they have constructed around themselves, empaths are prone to internalizing. This can compromise our shields and make it feel as though all of our solitary visualization work was for naught.

When we empaths first begin working with protective shields, it can feel as though even the slightest emotional altercation could destroy the shield and overturn all our hard work. This belief is strongly rooted in fear and a lack of self-confidence. Believe in yourself! Even if an unpleasant interaction or judgment gets through your shield, it's not the end of the world. Try, try again. Pick yourself back up and trust that you are doing the best you can to protect yourself emotionally.

When it feels like your protective shields have come tumbling down, please keep in mind that these shields can be *easily* reconstructed due to their astral imprint. When discussing this with fellow empaths, I always liken this process to the flame of a candle. When we blow out a flame, the wick continues to smoke for a short period of time. During this smoking phase, if we hold a match or lighter in the smoke right above the candle, even as high as an inch from the wick, the flame will "jump" back to the wick and reignite the candle. It's similar with our shields: if an experience compromises our shield—which it will from time to time—we can easily take a bit of space, do a bit of follow-up visualization, and discover that our shield has resurrected itself with relatively little effort—*and* we feel better as a result.

---

*Although empathic shielding and visualizations are extremely important, the truth is that empaths often have difficulty maintaining these energetic barriers. This is why an empath's most effective techniques of protection can take place during everyday social interactions.*

## *The Importance of Shielding*

Some empaths, psychics, healers, and other spiritualists prefer to construct energetic shields on a daily basis. It can be rewarding to perform a large ritual focused on energetic shielding, but it's not always necessary. When we awaken for the day, our consciousness is shifting from dreaming life to waking life. This gives us a good opportunity to invite some of the dreamier and more mystical energies into our waking reality. We can utilize this conscious "bridge" to our benefit by immediately slipping into meditation when we wake up. From here, we can easily direct our personal energies, which have been recharged from the sleeping process, to build or reinforce our protective shield. This is done by way of visualization.

When we visualize something in our mind's eye, that energy takes shape in its own way. The law of attraction is a common metaphysical understanding of the power of thought. By using visualization and *trusting* in our efforts, we can truly empower ourselves as co-creators of our own reality. Oftentimes, the effects of visualization can be experienced instantly. Because the mind and emotions are intricately linked, a calm mind helps influence calm emotions. Even if we do not choose to actively perform a visualization, the very process of meditation can have a profound effect on our mood.

Shielding is a process that can be as lengthy and intricate as you wish. Perhaps the most common method is to reserve a few minutes of meditation each day for the purpose of shielding. When visualizing the construction or reinforcement of your chosen shield, you are likely to fall back on a method of visualization that makes you feel comfortable and empowered. This is good; keep it up! Trust your intuition.

I have found that the ideal time to play with new shielding visualizations is when I'm feeling self-confident. Unfamiliar methods of visualization are fun to experiment with when we feel a sense of security because even a perceived "failed" attempt won't disrupt our general energy pattern. If I'm having a good day and decide to experiment with, say, creating a big bubble shield, but it feels too uncomfortable and floaty, I can easily "pop" this bubble to send it away without negatively impacting my mood.

Some shields are best constructed by drawing energy from both the cosmos above and the earth below. This Father Sky/ Mother Earth combination can create a unique energetic balance. Others find it effective to visualize certain energies, environments, materials, colors, frequencies, or spirit guides that can aid in the protective process. There is no right or wrong way to shield ourselves empathically.

Creative imagination is linked to the flow of energy and to both our psychic and our empathic level of functioning. Don't be afraid to use your imagination and see how you feel guided to craft effective shields of your liking. If you choose to construct your shields shortly after awakening from sleep, it's a good idea to take a few moments at the end of the day to review the effectiveness of each shield.

Finally, please don't become overly reliant on your shields. It's possible that you might find a low-intensity protective shield that works well for you on a daily basis, but don't panic if you forget to reconstruct it for a day or two. Go with the flow. There may be a number of days in which you don't feel the need to perform shielding, and that's okay! Many empaths and other sensitive souls prefer to practice shielding on an as-needed basis, but everyone's different.

*Everyday Empathic Techniques*

Feel free to experiment with different types of shields in different circumstances in order to find what works best for you in certain scenarios. Please be sure to *take down* your "old" shield when replacing it with a new visualization. Because shields create an astral imprint, we don't want to overload ourselves with potentially conflicting energies—we get enough of that in the real world!

Here are a few examples of potential shields that you can try visualizing. Please add to, expand, and clarify this list. Have fun experimenting to discover what works best for you!

- **Crystal shield:** For those of you who are interested in the metaphysical properties of gemstones, it can be a fun practice to experiment with the visualized construction of various crystals around your aura. As a general rule, if a type of stone has a somewhat transparent appearance, it is easier to visualize. The frequency of rose quartz differs from that of amethyst, for example, so I recommend physically experiencing different stones before visualizing their energetic construction. Most crystals are renowned for their protective and uplifting properties, so regularly visualizing a crystalline shield is believed to protect one's energy and simultaneously provide spiritual relief.

- **Egg shield:** The egg is one-half of the foundation for life. When we visualize ourselves surrounded by an egg, we create a semipermeable shield that protects us from external contaminants while still permitting a bit of breathing room. With ourselves situated as the embryo or yolk, the energy of spiritual nourishment is drawn into our person. This type of shield is especially beneficial when creating new beginnings and should be "broken" once a sense of internal breakthrough is achieved. Few shields feel as protective and comforting as the egg. The energy of this shield is both feminine and nurturing.

- **Mirror shield:** The mirror is one of the most common shields for psychics, empaths, and others who are frequently overwhelmed by external stimuli. While it may be tempting to wish to deflect everything but our own emotional energy, the regular use of a visualized mirror can in fact be distancing and make us energetically unrelatable to others. In certain difficult circumstances, a mirror shield can help keep us balanced and protected against overwhelming toxicity, but when used unnecessarily it can be alienating. Some practitioners like to attune the energy of their mirror shield to deflect only harmful energies while allowing the positive to enter.

- **Iron shield:** I include a mention of the iron shield here because of its danger. A shield of this type is advisable only temporarily and when the need feels dire. Any shield that visualizes an impenetrable structure is instantly isolating and should be utilized only under duress and quickly deconstructed once the problem is on its way to being resolved. When overused, a metallic shield can contribute to feelings of depression and isolation, so please be mindful if you ever choose to visualize this type of shield even briefly.

- **Cloak of invisibility:** As we learned at Hogwarts, a cloak of invisibility can help us avoid certain dangers. While not quite as glamorous as the fantastical depiction, an invisibility shield can help us go unnoticed when we need it most. Although it might be nice to think about becoming literally transparent, this type of shield is designed to help us blend in and avoid social contact when needed. This shield is for social situations and is strictly temporary. Please do not perform this type of shielding when walking, biking, or driving a motor vehicle, for safety reasons, or when at home alone; there is no reason to do so.

- **Coat of arms:** Every family or tribe has, at some point in history, utilized a coat of arms, totem, flag, emblem, or pattern to represent their heritage. Although a person's spiritual legacy is undoubtedly more significant than their genetic ancestry, there is a certain peace in connecting to one's heritage. Existential information and behaviors are often believed to be carried in a person's DNA, which is why the sacredness of one's bloodline continues to be a significant focus for many modern families. If you are able to discover the coat, crest, or other symbolic representation of at least one of your ancestral lineages, it may be worth experimenting with a visualization that constructs this symbol around your aura as a source of protection and confidence—and perhaps even a little boost of guidance from your ancestors.

- **Patterned shield:** It can be fun to experiment with shields that are patterned in some way. Whether it's covered in paisleys, diamonds, polka dots, or anything else under the sun, each patterned shield carries a different meaning. Through visualization, each pattern can be attuned to a specific protective purpose, depending on what each pattern means to you.

- **Empath's heart shield:** A unique method of empathic shielding is to draw energy from the heart chakra (Anahata) outward to surround the body. Because empaths live from the heart, it makes sense to extend this energy to create a protective form. This opening of the heart can also help empaths stay connected to others with peaceful and loving energies throughout the day. This type of shield is ideal for circumstances in which you foresee positive social interactions with a minimum potential for conflict. This shield should ideally be visualized in an emerald-green color.

- **Shield of prayer:** Prayer of any type can assist us in feeling surrounded by protective and encouraging forces. Whether we call upon spirit guides, angels, God, gods, goddesses, ancestors, saints, gurus, ascended masters, or anyone else, the effects of prayer-based protection can be easily felt and experienced throughout the day. This type of shielding does not necessarily require an additional visualized shield per se, but it can accompany other such shields if desired.

- **Elemental shield:** Most mystical systems recognize four physical elements: earth, air, fire, and water. A powerful method of protection is to invite the energy of an element into your space for protective purposes. Visualize the element surrounding your aura. You may feel guided to visualize flowers and ferns surrounding you, or perhaps a placid ocean or waterfall. Elemental shields of protection are highly creative, and each element can be aligned with a different purpose. Earth-based visualizations can provide grounding, air-based visualizations can aid the intellect, fire-based visualizations can increase energy, and water-based visualizations can provide empathic connection and protection.

## Navigating Adversity

Social conflicts suck, and the vast majority of empaths do everything they can to avoid them. But life isn't always sunshine and rainbows and unicorns, especially for empaths. Let's be realistic: as much as we'd like to think of ourselves as being compassionate and calm and collected at all times of the day, this isn't always the case. Maybe such a state of being is the ideal or goal, but in reality there are times when we're anything but warm and fuzzy. This is not always the result of other people's negativity wearing off on us, although at times this can most definitely be a huge factor.

We have our own shit to deal with, and so does everyone else on the planet. Whether we think of life's challenges as circumstances, life lessons, or karma, we must face, accept, understand, and come to terms with them.

## *Interpersonal Negativity*

Now that we've explored some techniques for dealing with confusing emotions on a personal level, let's explore some of the challenges of interacting with negativity from other individuals.

During difficult social interactions, whether in person, on the phone, online, or through written communication, it's important to remember that you are emotionally sensitive. You are likely to feel the emotions that the other person is projecting. Your first instinct will likely be to mirror or absorb those emotions and to link those sensations to your own related emotional landscape. If the other person is feeling angry, the interaction is likely to trigger your *own* internal anger. If you are feeling emotionally weak, the other person's anger could give rise to a reactionary response of sadness and self-pity. In psychology, this is called *emotional countercontagion*.

Everyday empathy requires us to discover our own methods of dealing with external rushes of negativity, because they *do* happen from time to time. That's life! When we know which responses work best for us in certain situations, we can learn to resolve a situation more quickly than we would if we were blindsided.

Many psychologists recommend using "I feel" responses during difficult interactions, especially if the other person is a close friend or life partner. Slinging accusations and insults at the other person will probably only cause the negativity to snowball. By bringing your own part of the conversation back to feelings and emotional awareness, you encourage the other party to do the same. Also try incorporating emotion-based observations of the other person, such as "I realize you are upset," but be careful not to sound patronizing.

If you're overwhelmed, shift your body slightly away from the other person so you are not fully immersed in their energy (or hold the phone slightly away from your ear). Take longer breaks from eye contact so you can mentally process the information. But remain balanced; you don't want to totally break eye contact or you may appear disinterested.

When you realize that a conflict is occurring, it's wise to remember that we empaths have the responsibility to transmute and transform energies. We are capable of feeling an emotion and shifting it to a higher frequency. For more information about this, please see the section "The Ins and Outs of Emotional Energy" at the beginning of chapter 2.

There are times when our interactions with others will feel less than pleasant. It's up to us to discern when an interaction is worth continuing and when it's time to take a break. It's my hope that you, as an empath, choose to surround yourself only with individuals who also demonstrate high levels of empathy. It can be deflating and unfulfilling to spend time with people who regularly engage in criticism, social judgment, selfishness, apathy, addiction, and other detrimental modes of functioning.

Although it may feel natural to forgive and forget even the most abhorrent behavior in others, it's not always in that person's best interest or your own to do so. By practicing emotional discernment and choosing to be brave enough to call people out by sharing a much-needed perspective, we can actually help increase *their* self-awareness while also boosting our own conversational confidence.

It can be confusing to feel anger toward another person. Much of the time, this is justifiable and takes some clear communication to work through. I also want to let you in on a bit of wisdom that greatly helps cultivate empathy and compassion toward another person with whom you are having difficulty, and that is to realize that they, much like you, have experienced deep sorrow in their past. By cultivating compassion toward the part of the other person that has also felt this pain of existence, it becomes much easier to create a bridge of compassionate communication.

Remember, you don't need to please everyone in your life at all times. It's okay to disagree—in fact, it can be quite healthy. Disagreements and challenging social interactions don't have to be black marks of negativity, but can give rise to productive conversations and deeper levels of healing when approached with respect for yourself and others.

It's also important to mention that we empaths are usually some of the last people to realize when we are involved in an emotionally abusive situation. Recently, I witnessed a man and his wife at a hardware store. He was making the most horrible, degrading, and belittling statements to her in the next aisle. My heart went out to her because she was just smiling and nodding, although I sensed a deep sadness and emotional longing within her—understandably so! I was revolted by this exchange and actually mustered the courage to confront him by saying, "Please don't talk to people like that." His dismissive response to me once again framed her in a degrading light, and he walked away to avoid facing accountability. I secretly performed some instant energy work on her (which also helped me avoid absorbing the negative energy of the situation) and later prayed for her soul to recognize this person's danger so that she might find the self-confidence to disconnect herself from this abuse. I instantly recognized the woman in this scenario as an empath who, rather than fighting for her rights, had surrendered to an emotionally violent situation.

The realization of the toxicity of this situation was reason enough for me to send out some serious bursts of white light with healing intentions. This is because I believe that certain situations don't necessarily require the recipient's express permission for prayer or energetic work, especially if the intention being sent is focused solely on healing light. Who doesn't want a bit of that? Being an empathic lightworker requires a suspension of judgment in order to send pure and gentle universal energy to those in need.

I hope the story of this experience will help empathic readers who find themselves in an abusive or humiliating situation with a partner, family members, friends, colleagues, or anyone else. Empaths are *not* designed to be punching bags for others, and there is *always* help available. Protect yourself, respect yourself, and love yourself.

### Everyday Empathic Techniques

It feels uncomfortable to be overtaken by emotional energy. Regardless of its point of origin, emotional overload must be dealt with as quickly as possible. There is no sense wallowing in negative feelings, even when we can't find it within ourselves to cope in any other way. When we get proactive—and when we allow for spiritual trust and hope to enter the picture—we can more easily process emotional overload and come to a place of understanding.

When we feel angry, upset, discombobulated, or otherwise flustered, here are a few ideas to help us regain our balance:

- **Recognize the feeling:** First and foremost, bring mindful awareness to the fact that you are presently experiencing an emotional challenge. Realize this, recognize this, and become aware of your surroundings.

- **Accept the emotions:** Acceptance does not imply submission. Instead, it's wise to accept the fact that you are feeling something unpleasant. If you're unable to solve the dilemma immediately, simply accept the fact that you are navigating a challenge and affirm that you desire to alleviate this suffering in a productive way.

- **Take a break:** If possible, disengage from any external stimuli that may be contributing to your current state. If it would be helpful to lie down for a minute, go for it. If you're in public, perhaps a quick trip to the bathroom would give you time to take some deep breaths. If there are external contributors, remove yourself from the trigger temporarily in order to regroup your energy. Take the time you need to calm down and come back to center.

- **Higher self-awareness:** Remember that you are not your emotions. The brain receives sensations and responds accordingly, incorporating the emotional and physical bodies in the process. Remember that you are spirit; you are energy. Although your soul may be inhabiting this body vehicle for this lifetime, the higher self transcends these limitations and is intricately connected to everyone and everything in existence—including whatever may be contributing to your stress. This cognitive act of separation is not a means to escape what you are feeling but rather is a way to more deeply engage by regaining sight of the bigger picture.

- **Explore the sensation:** If you feel comfortable enough to explore the sensations you are feeling, try meditating and focusing on the feelings themselves. Do you have emotions on top of other emotions, such as anger as a response to fear? Could there be triggers from the past that are contributing to your emotions feeling heavier than they really need to be at this time? Try recognizing these feelings for what they are. If these feelings are ongoing and burdensome, consider seeing a counselor or therapist to assist with the emotions. There are times when we all deserve this, and we are all very lucky to have access to mental health treatment.

- **Consider the origin:** Do you feel as though this negative flurry of emotions is coming from within you, or is it the result of absorbing external negativity? To be honest, most of the time it doesn't really matter; it's more important to process what you're feeling in the moment so you can regain your balance and sense of confidence. If you feel like the origin of the emotion is important, be sure not to play the blame game with yourself or anyone else. We are all in this together, and stress is oftentimes the result of numerous factors.

- **Cleanse yourself:** Do whatever it takes to come back to balance, whether by taking a bath, petting an animal, smudging yourself with sage, having a glass of wine (or a puff!), taking a nap, listening to relaxing music, meditating, or doing anything else with which you personally resonate.

## Exercise: *Self-Limitation Cord Cutting*

Empaths tend to be experts at creating stress even when it's unnecessary. Believe me, I know how easy it is to get worked up about even the smallest detail. I know how it feels to blow things out of proportion and create a sense of panic even when everything is okay. I know how easy it is to fear the future. Empaths are notorious for second-guessing themselves, so it only makes sense that we are prone to believe that other people hold the same level of criticism toward us personally.

Self-limiting beliefs are just that: self-created ideas about ourselves that actually serve no purpose besides sabotaging our confidence. These limitations are, in fact, actually life lessons in disguise. It's up to us to journey into these fears and insecurities, especially when these imprints have been created as a result of past experiences. These limitations are actually opportunities to learn more about ourselves and our place in the world.

In this exercise, readers are encouraged to perform a bit of proactive healing centered around past incidents. The "past," in this sense, can consist of experiences in childhood or even things that happened only yesterday. Performing this exercise can help us release harmful self-imposed beliefs that hinder deeper emotional development. Honest self-examination is not the easiest thing in the world, but it encourages us to be realistic and gain a more objective perspective of our experiences.

This exercise is best performed during a full moon or at any time during the moon's waning cycle. Some readers will identify this exercise as a "spell" of sorts. In many ways this is true, because magickal work is a process of altering one's consciousness to align with a spiritual intention. This is similar to psychological work aimed at transforming negative thinking and its resulting behavioral patterns.

As always, please do this exercise at your own pace and feel free to perform it multiple times as your intuition dictates. There is no pressure to do it perfectly. Again, intuition is your best guide when it comes to emotionally transformative work. I encourage you to be proud of yourself for taking steps toward personal healing. Goodness knows we all could use a bit of self-healing on a regular basis!

1. For this exercise, procure a stack of blank paper, a permanent marker, scissors, and a full roll of all-natural string or twine. Once you have these components assembled, situate yourself in a private space where you will not be disturbed for at least an hour. Planning is important here because the assurance of privacy is a matter of emotional safety when navigating potentially vulnerable levels of the psyche.

2. Be sure that you are in a good emotional and mental state of mind before beginning this exercise; this will safeguard your energy and allow you to more easily examine emotional imprints from an objective place. I recommend that you sit in a chair or on the floor, perhaps in front of your altar if you have one. Make your environment as comfortable as possible. It is essential that you feel peaceful and spiritually protected. Calm yourself. Perform any protective exercises or prayers to spirits, gods, or ancestors that you deem appropriate. Do what feels right in order to feel balanced, comfortable, and safe.

3. With the marker and paper, begin by writing harmful self-limiting beliefs that you have experienced throughout your life. Consider various insecurities that have led to moments when you've had a low self-image. Write each of these harmful beliefs on a separate page. This can include anything from "I will always be rejected" to "I am not attractive enough." Pay special attention to self-limiting beliefs that are comparisons between yourself and others. Are these your genuine feelings or are they manifestations of harsh social expectations?

4. Take some time to write down these insecurities; there is no rush. Meditate and search your mind for self-limiting viewpoints that may have caused you to feel socially isolated in childhood or young adulthood and beliefs that may still be present in your everyday experience. As you record these points, remember that these are *fears*. They are not accurate assessments of your character. Do your best to separate yourself emotionally from these expressions, because this is the first step in cutting the attachments between these beliefs and your true self.

5. When you feel like you have expressed all of the horrible and self-deprecating ideas that you can muster, take some deep breaths and envision the pages as entities that are separate from yourself. Look at the pages of ideas and verbally tell them why they no longer serve your spirit. These are not *you*; they are limitations that you have allowed to taint your happiness. Many of these fears are the result of you absorbing social judgments and passing criticisms. They are not you.

6. Once you feel a sense of separation from these beliefs, cut a length of string or twine approximately five to eight feet long. Tie one end around your left wrist (the left represents the past), and place the other end atop the first piece of paper. Out loud, read the insecurity that you wrote on this page. Take a moment to think about what it says, and allow your mind to be filled with the knowledge that this was a belief that you allowed into your emotional body due to past experiences. It is likely that you will recall some instances that contributed to these awful thoughts. If this occurs, focus the energy of these experiences into the words on the paper. You are in a protected spiritual space, so it's necessary to separate yourself from these emotions in the moment. Cry if you feel the need to.

7. When you feel as though you have come to terms with the words written on the page, be sure to *smile* at the fact that you're seeing these self-imposed limitations for what they are. Choose to celebrate the fact that you are actively releasing these emotions in a healthy and constructive way. Affirm that you are ready to learn the lessons held within these beliefs and that you are ready to begin the process of releasing these fears once and for all.

8. To affirm the separation between you and the self-limiting belief, forcefully *spit* on the page and immediately crumple it, with the string attached. Drop the crumpled piece of paper on the floor, noticing that the paper is still attached to your left wrist by the cord.

9. Repeat this process for every piece of paper that you wrote on. Take some time with this exercise. By performing this exercise, you are declaring to the universe that you are a

sacred spiritual being who deserves healing in order to help yourself and others in life.

10. When you have performed this exercise with every piece of paper, take some time to ground and center yourself. Congratulate yourself for having the courage to face these emotional wounds.

11. In an act of bravery, verbally declare that you are choosing to separate yourself from these horrible belief patterns. Take the scissors in your right hand and *cut* the cords that bind you to these pieces of paper. If you think that crying or yelling would be cathartic while you snip the cords, go for it!

12. Throw the cords to the ground, then stand up and envision yourself surrounded by a healing white light that comes from Mother Earth below and Father Sky above. Smile, take some deep breaths, and thank the universe for this experience. Finish by either throwing the pages and cords in the trash or burning them in a bonfire. Follow your intuition.

13. As you go about your daily life, you are likely to be reminded of these insecurities on a regular basis. Do your best to nip these thoughts in the bud. When depressive and anxious thoughts threaten to invade your emotional body, recognize their origins in these self-limiting beliefs. When this occurs in the future, mentally send these dark energies to the pages that you've discarded. Healing is a process, and you are well on your way to achieving greater energetic balance to carry you through anything life throws in your direction.

chapter four

# An Empath's Natural Cycles & Rhythms

Empaths can be considered HSPs: highly sensitive persons. However, it's important to note that if someone is an HSP, it does not necessarily make them an empath. Many individuals who demonstrate emotional sensitivity do not actually exercise much empathy in daily life. HSPs of all stripes can be emotionally influenced by the world around them, and this extends well beyond the social sphere.

The experience of empathy itself is greatly social, but we are also affected by other cycles and shifts in our surroundings. We find ourselves here on earth, zooming through the vastness of space at an orbit of twenty miles per second around the sun, and additionally rotating at a rate of a thousand miles an hour—aren't those some dizzying figures?

As the earth orbits and rotates, our paradise of a planet is influenced by interactions with other planetary bodies in a grand cosmic dance. In many ways, we are subject to the whims and changes of nature. In truth, it's not we who are in control; we're just along for the ride.

## Daily Energy Shifts

When a new day is born every twenty-four hours, we are given an opportunity to realign ourselves with the cycles and rhythms of nature and therefore with our own personal cycles and rhythms.

In the next chapter, I will be discussing the importance of sleep when it comes to positive empathic functioning. For now, let it be said that making time for proper sleep is of the utmost importance when it comes to our daily cycles. The cycle of sleep allows us to rejuvenate our energy, repair tissue, and sort out our psyche by way of dreaming. When we wake up each restful morning, we get to choose which vibrations to align ourselves with for the day's adventure.

### The Everyday Cycle

It's a wise idea for empaths to track their emotional energies throughout the various phases of the day's cycle. For some, it is beneficial to keep a journal to jot down observations of these shifts on any given day.

Everyone has a different daily cycle. When bringing awareness to your energy levels on a daily basis, it's worth noticing how your energy is maintained on a typical workday versus on a day off, or how your energy changes on days when you have a lot of social obligations versus on days when you get to go read a book in the park. Beyond the obligations of the daily grind, notice how different people and different social dynamics affect your emotional state. For us empaths, sometimes all it takes is interacting with one negative person to send us into an emotional tailspin.

And while we have the ability to choose not to respond in this way, it's worth noting that we experienced something with that potential.

Before you hit the day socially, take note of where your energy is at. There are times when you'll find yourself influenced by the weather (hooray for sunny days!) and other times when you'll find yourself influenced by your dreams. Bring awareness to your emotional body as you start your day. Depending on how you're feeling, you may wish to perform meditation, prayer, devotion, an exercise from this book, or something else to get you in a positive state. As you may come to notice, the emotions with which you begin your morning can set the stage for the entire day's emotional experience.

Throughout the day, our energies, emotions, and thoughts will naturally shift and fluctuate. These cycles are normal in moderation, and it's essential for us to objectively track any shifts. See how you feel as you get going for the day. Check in with yourself at midday, in the afternoon, in the evening, and at night. Pay particular attention to how each phase influences your emotions.

Personally—and maybe it's because I'm such a Goth—I've discovered that even if I have a day of energetic depletion, my energy and mood *always* become a bit lighter after nightfall. As a result, when I'm feeling stressed or discombobulated in the daytime, I look forward to becoming realigned when the sun goes down.

When it comes to analyzing how the day's cycles influence your energy, take it a step further by examining the details: Which emotions have people around you displayed today? Could you have absorbed some of these feelings without realizing it?

Additionally, think about the tasks and activities you experienced today. Did something in particular uplift or exhaust your energy?

With enough attention to detail, we can see how each step in the day affects us as empaths, and we can determine to what extent the daily sun cycle affects us versus the extent to which our everyday interactions and activities have an effect.

---

*Throughout the day, our energies, emotions,*
*and thoughts will naturally shift and fluctuate.*
*These cycles are normal in moderation, and it's*
*essential for us to objectively track any shifts.*
*See how you feel as you get going for the day.*
*Check in with yourself at midday, in the afternoon,*
*in the evening, and at night. Pay particular attention*
*to how each phase influences your emotions.*

### The Empath and Sexuality

In addition to the hormone-influenced phases of the human life cycle, it is of great importance for empaths to be mindful of their own daily sexual cycle. I've come to understand that, at least for me, sexual energy regenerates after a night's sleep. This energetic regeneration seems to be common among those who have "boy parts."

For those who experience menstrual cycles, it can be deeply empowering to bring awareness and intention to this cyclical occurrence. Oftentimes this sort of tracking is helpful by way of journaling and empathetic social support.

People who identify as transgender, third-gender, or gender-queer also face their own sets of challenges. Whereas many ancient (and modern) cultures across the world understand and value the magic of non-binary souls, modern puritanical culture has done much to suppress, oppress, and brutalize gender-based notions that appear different from the norm. Individuals who straddle gender polarities have a unique and very sacred, even shamanic, place in the world.

Individuals of all genders have different preferences, callings, and libidos. Modern societies around the world often seem to place an excessive emphasis on sex in general, which can lead to numerous social and psychological pressures if a person isn't willing to separate their own feelings from unhealthy social groupthink. Empaths of all stripes must strive to take control of their own sexuality and its expression. One of the most important factors in this is the elimination of *shame.*

Sexual shame can arise for countless reasons, including childhood trauma, bullying, sexual violence, abusive relationships, and inconsiderate social norms. Personally, if I engage in sexual activity, including masturbation, I am very careful to express this powerful energy in only positive, loving, and compassionate ways. Empaths have a tendency to personalize difficult experiences, so it is vital that we maintain a positive relationship with our own sexual views and expressions. When it comes to romantic interactions with others, I like to remember the Wiccan phrase "perfect love and perfect trust." When these things are present between consenting adults, anything is possible—both inside and outside the bedroom!

I can empathize with many readers about these issues. I've long struggled with my own matters of shame related to sex and intimacy. Since puberty, a shadowy part of my consciousness has needled my mind with the idea that I "should be heterosexual." I believe these shame-related issues have their roots in teenage bullying and in the observation of social norms. Additionally, I feel that some of these shame-related imprints (and therefore life lessons) were karmically borne of choices made in past lives. We empaths must be true to our hearts, even when it feels challenging.

As someone born and raised in the United States, I can say that views on sexuality, gender, and relationship models are thankfully quite liberal here compared to those in much of the world. While it may seem like an uphill battle to come to terms with your own identities (even if they *are* the norm), our empathetic acts of compassion help influence others in the world to live with greater confidence.

An empath's sex life should also be viewed with compassion. Whether you engage in regular sex and/or masturbation or you feel more asexual, you must maintain a healthy relationship with sexual energy in general. I have found myself coming to terms with sexual concerns by researching various aspects of sex, gender, and intimacy. Education is empowerment. Everyone on earth has a different relationship to sexual energy, and the science of sexuality is still in its infancy. With every passing year, we make new discoveries in this important field of study.

According to innumerable modern studies, both gender and sexuality are in fact one giant continuum—a spectrum. These *natural* and *normal* variations have existed for as long as humans have walked the earth. Not only that, but personal identifications and proclivities along this spectrum can actually change to some degree throughout the course of a person's life. I believe that this also holds true across multiple lifetimes and reincarnations. While labels and identities can provide a sense of comfort and community, I feel that it is very important for empaths to be open to variations in gender and sexuality in both themselves and others.

We empaths often take social norms and criticisms on board when assessing our own self-worth. This often happens on a subconscious level, which is why it's deeply important for us to examine past experiences and come to terms with ourselves in the present. Like any other tool of transformation, sexuality can be used for both good and evil. By embracing love toward others and ourselves, in terms of both sexuality and life in general, we can help energetically influence the world to be a place of kindness rather than violence, one step at a time. We all deserve love, no matter who we are, what we've done, or what we've experienced.

We have the opportunity to love ourselves, regardless of our sexual or gender identity and our past experiences. We have the opportunity to *own* and *protect* our sexual energy rather than cave to social expectations or succumb to sexual manipulations of others—an all-too-common experience for highly empathic souls (especially women). Sexuality deserves to be celebrated as a positive, loving, and bonding force—one of the most powerful expressions of love on the physical plane. If we feel damaged in these areas, we must do everything we can to heal these imprints and develop a healthy relationship to gender and sexuality.

———

*We empaths often take social norms and criticisms on board when assessing our own self-worth. This often happens on a subconscious level, which is why it's deeply important for us to examine past experiences and come to terms with ourselves in the present.*

## Planetary and Astrological Cycles

A part of the empath's heart lies in nature, in the natural rhythm of the world around us. We may frequently find ourselves influenced by the lunar and solar cycles of waxing and waning light. Those of us who are attuned to the cycles of astrology may track changes in our mood and personality (and those of the people around us) as indicated by planetary movements.

### The Sun

As every empath knows, we are highly susceptible to changes in the energy in our environment. One of the most well-known examples of change occurs when there is less sunlight during the day. With the winter solstice being the longest night of the year (and thus having the shortest period of daylight), many empaths and sensitive souls find themselves withdrawing into melancholy during the colder months.

Seasonal affective disorder (SAD) is a very real phenomenon that has a palpable effect on many people's moods and perspectives. It is reassuring to see how common light therapy is becoming and how many people actively recognize and work with depressive cycles based in seasonal (solar) fluctuations.

It is important for empaths to understand how their own moods and emotional energies shift with each season. For this reason, it's a good idea to keep a journal where you can keep track of emotional patterns connected to the seasonal shifts. For example, I have long found myself feeling the most depressed in the summertime and the most exuberant in the autumn. It really is different for every empath!

### The Moon

For many empaths, the moon also plays a big role in their daily emotions. Some empaths find themselves invigorated and inspired when the full moon rides high in the sky, and some say that the new moon is a time of great introspection and reflection. In esoteric systems, both the full moon and the new moon are times to honor the divine feminine and focus on personal prayer.

It is believed that the waning moon is a time to focus on banishing or dismissing unwanted energies, while the waxing moon is a time of attracting and summoning positive forces to aid us in life's journey.

Take note of how each lunar cycle affects your energy. Because life's daily emotions are influenced by *so many* factors and dynamics, it's very important to come to your own conclusions regarding the extent to which your mood is affected by the phase of the moon, versus the time of year, time of day, astrological configurations, and other potential factors.

### The Cosmos

When discussing nature's influence on empaths, it would be folly of me to neglect mentioning astrology. Many metaphysically minded individuals are drawn to astrological interpretations to help explain the ebbs and flows of life, as well as their own personal strengths and limitations.

While Vedic astrology and numerous other systems exist, most people are familiar with traditional Western "tropical" astrology. At this point in time, a number of astrological arts have merged, cross-pollinated, and shared wisdom as cultures have developed and intermingled.

Astrology is not quite as cut-and-dried as it may appear in the horoscope section of the newspaper. Numerous factors are at play in a person's natal chart, and each person is influenced in a different way by the transits of cosmic bodies.

Empaths function primarily from their emotional body, sensing and feeling everything on a deeper level than the majority of folks. It's reasonable to think that empaths and other psychics are especially influenced by planetary tides, which is why it can be invaluable to gain insight into our own unique astrological blueprint. Many experienced astrologers are available to cast a person's birth chart and provide a meaningful interpretation. Most of these individuals can be found online, and it's likely that you have professional astrologers in your own local area, even if you live in a small town.

It should also be mentioned that it can be tempting to blame one's own issues on a zodiac chart or planetary shift (Mercury retrograde, anyone?). Although these conditions may be influential factors, we all have a personal responsibility to remain realistic about our *own* internal cosmic conditions. After all, each of us is at the center of our own universe.

### The Zodiac

The following is a brief list of the common tropical zodiac signs in Western astrology, with a special focus on the emotional influence of each sign. Because astrological shifts influence every empath in a different way, I am able to provide only a general overview of the empathetic energies associated with each sign. There is *much* more to the art and science of astrology than I can possibly communicate in these pages, though I do find it helpful to present general information that can be accepted or more deeply explored by each individual reader. The information included here is basic; even a person who only knows "their sign" (sun sign) can reflect on how it influences their life as an empath.

Simple, everyday astrological shifts can also be reflected upon as well. Many people are aware of when the planets Venus and Mercury are visible in the night sky and when the Sun enters a particular zodiac sign. (The Sun enters the sign of Libra at the autumnal equinox, for example.) Metaphysical folks are often aware of their Moon sign, rising sign (Ascendant), and other natal configurations. Regardless of the extent of your astrological knowledge, it's helpful to pay attention to how the planets and signs are shifting around us.

- **Aries:** This zodiacal influence is enthusiastic, thriving on new beginnings and fresh starts. Emotionally, Aries is connected to the fiery force of change. When Aries is exercising an influence, expect empathy to be highlighted best when there is a newfound sense of transformation occurring on an emotional level. At times this energy of emotional dynamism comes from the completion of projects, from new social experiences, or from newfound levels of personal healing.

- **Taurus:** Being a more slow-to-change influence, the earthy and methodical energy of Taurus is rooted in consistency and reliability. Taurus is a sign of loyalty and inner strength. Empaths can benefit from Taurus's emotional lesson of "slow and steady wins the race." Love in its many forms can easily be said to fall under the domain of Taurus, which is why this energy can be so empathically beneficial. Taurus also teaches us to do our own work as empaths rather than relying on other people's perspectives.

- **Gemini:** Exercising an influence that is more psychic than empathic, Gemini's airy energy can help empaths think rationally and consider different perspectives. Because empaths often take things too seriously, we are at risk of getting lost in internal loops of emotional stress. Gemini can help with this, with its more lighthearted influence. Represented by two people, the cosmic twins, and due to its rulership by the planet Mercury, Gemini energy is very communicative and can assist us in improving our interpersonal skills.

- **Cancer:** Being one of the three water signs, Cancer energy is highly emotional and somewhat introverted. Emotional safety is most definitely a theme exemplified by Cancer the crab. Empaths can greatly benefit from Cancer's protective energy. This sign's energy is open to change, but not without first taking any necessary precautions. Cancer's emotional energy is said to be cautiously optimistic. This slight level of emotional distance can help us rein in tendencies of emotional carelessness.

- **Leo:** Fiery Leo's empathic qualities are greatly based in self-assuredness. This confidence can take the form of public approval but truly shines when it comes from within. Leo is a sign of warmth and compassion, and its influence can be inspirational for empathic souls who are in need of some love, laughter, and loyalty. Due to Leo's connection to the ego, this sign's influence can also be positive by helping define the "self." This is significant considering that empaths are sometimes quick to lose their own identity in a rush of absorbed emotions.

- **Virgo:** Both intelligent and meticulous, Virgo's earthy energy is sharp and focused. Although it has a tendency to be worrisome and overcritical, this sign can aid empaths with problem solving. This mental acuteness can be of great value to those who easily miss the emotional forest for the trees. Additionally, Virgo lends an influence of emotional adaptability, allowing rational thinking to take the place of emotional stagnation.

- **Libra:** As the symbol of the scales of balance, airy Libra is focused on adjustment and balance, both cosmically and personally. Libra teaches lessons focused on the importance of emotional equilibrium. As a sign of amicability, Libra can help empaths socially by encouraging peaceful, respectful, and emotionally healthy exchanges. Libra reminds us of the importance of emotional, mental, and physical wellbeing.

- **Scorpio:** Scorpio energy is renowned for its intensity and force. This sign can help us get in touch with our deepest emotions, encouraging self-examination to help heal emotional imprints, social conditioning, and traumas from the past. Scorpio has a highly intuitive energy that aids empaths on their journey of finding themselves. Scorpio embodies a deep well of emotional energy that is simply incomparable across the zodiac.

- **Sagittarius:** Inspiration can be gained from the expansive vibrations of Sagittarius, a sign of growth and experience. The archer's fiery arrow can help us push against our limits in constructive ways, instilling a sense of optimism and free-spiritedness, of which introverted empaths are often so greatly in need. Sagittarian energy helps us think things through and open ourselves to all the world has to offer, helping us to view life through the eyes of others.

- **Capricorn:** As an earth sign, Capricorn can help us ground our energies and accomplish our goals. Capricorn helps us focus on what is important in *our* lives and examine and recognize our personal accomplishments. Capricorn's influence reminds us of the success that comes from heartfelt dedication and purposeful self-discipline, rather than being swept along by other's whims.

- **Aquarius:** Although its symbol is the water bearer, Aquarius is actually an air sign. This dichotomy makes sense considering Aquarius's unique and creative nature. Perhaps the most eccentric of the zodiac signs, Aquarius encourages us to take the lead and create our own reality, and not simply follow the herd. This sign teaches us lessons of emotional independence and the need for inventive thinking. Aquarius also lends an energy of assistance when it comes to emotional expression and the creative arts.

- **Pisces:** A watery sign of great empathetic capacity, Pisces helps us connect with the internal and external flow of empathic energy in daily life. Pisces helps us connect with the emotional needs of others while at the same time discovering methods of personal emotional healing. This sign is emotionally mutable, flexible, and flowing and can assist us in "moving on" when we find ourselves clinging to the side of an emotional riverbank. Pisces teaches us lessons of emotional safety and compassion in action.

### The Planets

Throughout time and across cultures, the planetary bodies surrounding the earth have been believed to each have a certain energetic influence. When looking at astrological systems, we see that zodiac signs are "ruled" by specific planets. Each one has a different effect on us as empaths. Depending on how well versed you are in astrological studies, this planetary information can be applied to something as complex as a natal chart or to something as simple as noticing that Venus is visible on today's horizon.

- **Sun:** Being the center of our solar system, the Sun represents the sustenance of life and the power of change. The Sun as a physical planet activates life on this planet, sustaining existence and allowing us all to thrive. From the vantage point of the earth, the Sun transits through the signs of the zodiac, so it's wise for empaths to be aware of these transitions and come to conclusions about the influence of these shifts. The Sun is also symbolic of the masculine/projective energy, the ego, and self-identity, which are valuable qualities for empaths to invoke, helping us become more secure in our identity instead of merely going by the assessments of others.

- **Moon:** In metaphysical systems worldwide, the Moon represents the internal landscape. Being the silent and gorgeous satellite we all observe in the night sky, Lady Luna travels through each zodiac sign (usually every few days) from our vantage point on earth. It can be valuable for empaths to pay attention to which sign the Moon is in at any given time, as this can help us understand how the signs can influence our deepest emotions. The Moon in its various aspects—waxing, waning, full, and new—has various symbolic qualities and represents the power of change, particularly emotional change.

- **Earth:** The gorgeous planet we call home is the centerpiece of it all. It's easy to get caught up in the energetic influences of the cosmic bodies, but it's equally important to ground ourselves to the rhythm of nature. We can ground the macrocosmic views of the universe into the microcosm of terrestrial living. By paying attention to the cycles and patterns of the natural world, we can become more aware of synchronicities and life lessons playing out in our everyday existence.

- **Mercury:** Mercury is the planet that moves the fastest around the Sun. For this reason, Mercury is often considered to be the messenger planet, who quickly communicates information. Aligned with numerous deities across ancient mythical systems, Mercury is said to oversee communication, technology, and scientific fields of study. Mercury's fast-paced and intellectual energy can help us examine our emotions from an objective point of view.

- **Venus:** Oh Venus, luscious planet of love! Venusian energy is particularly appealing to empathic souls because it reminds us that love is the guide for life; without love, we cannot progress as a culture or as individuals. It is by valuing love in all its forms that we can create a deep gratitude for life's blessings, even during tumultuous times. Venusian energy is harmonizing, helping us balance life's ups and downs and encouraging compassion both for ourselves and for others.

- **Mars:** Renowned as a planet of assertiveness and sometimes even aggression or war, Mars energy sometimes feels like the antithesis of empathy. In reality, Mars energy is also very passionate, creative, and productive and can inspire even the most introspective of souls to lift up our heads and take the steps needed to accomplish our goals, even if we feel like giving in to stagnation.

- **Jupiter:** A planet of growth and expansion, Jupiter is also renowned as a bringer of luck and illumination. Empathic souls are often in need of inspiration to embrace personal growth, and Jupiter is masterful at assisting with the desire to achieve goals of all types. Embodying a highly optimistic energy, Jupiter assists empaths in bursting through stagnation and remembering our purpose here on earth.

- **Saturn:** Though Saturn is sometimes viewed as an unlucky planet, its energy is actually quite beneficial for those who are embarking on inner journeys and seeking personal healing. Saturn's energy influences us to look within and examine our own insecurities, fears, and limitations. Additionally, Saturn's energy helps us invoke the self-discipline and self-awareness needed to get the hard work done and be successful.

- **Uranus:** One of the three "outer planets" unknown to classical astrologers (though recognized in modern Western astrology), Uranus is all about new beginnings in life. The energy of Uranus is revolutionary and individualistic, encouraging empaths and other sensitive souls to embrace their uniqueness and be okay with being different. Uranus helps illuminate our inner light and reminds us of our significance in the dance of life.

- **Neptune:** Aligned with various oceanic deities, watery Neptune is highly emotional, aligning significantly with both empathy and psychicism. Neptune's influence is dreamy—sometimes escapist—and allows us to consider tendencies we may have toward emotional escapism and illusory thinking. Neptune helps us discern fact from fiction, especially when it comes to empathically internalizing external emotions through our own unique filter of experience.

- **Pluto:** Although demoted to "dwarf planet" status in 2006, Pluto is still believed to influence life on earth. Being the outermost planetary body in our solar system (to the best of our knowledge!), Pluto is naturally "big" in terms of its influence on life and death, destruction and resurrection. Pluto reminds us to step outside our own limited viewpoint and see the bigger picture. By doing this, empaths are reminded of what is truly important since everything in life will change, transform, die, and—in some manner—be reborn.

## *Exercise:* Morning and Evening Rituals for Empaths

When we awaken for the day, we find that the emotional energies of the previous day have settled down a bit. This is greatly due to the experience of dreaming, which bridges the conscious and unconscious minds. When we wake up, we can approach the day with a relatively fresh start. When we begin our morning, it's essential as empaths to set an intention for the day. This intention creates a vibration that can help carry us through the day until we once again lay our head down to rest.

Aligning the body, mind, and spirit as an intentional act is very beneficial for people of all sensitivity levels. For those who operate primarily on the mental or intellectual plane, an intentional morning routine can create a psychological framework by which they can direct their thoughts and daily focus. Those of us who demonstrate high emotional sensitivity can discover that movement such as physical (hatha) yoga can provide a much-needed boost of energy that helps us become more grounded for the day. We empathic individuals can find that our emotions and personal energies default to a more balanced state when we consistently align our thoughts with optimism at the start of each day.

Everyone is affected by the daily solar cycle and the sun's seasonal cycle. We can observe these shifts in our energy at these specific times and can choose to align ourselves to the natural chemical shifts that occur within us as the sunlight changes throughout the day and throughout the year.

I've always noticed that my general energy level shifts at dusk. When nighttime falls, our energies become more internalized; it makes sense that our minds can most easily process experiences under a shroud of stars. Just the same, the dawn of sunrise has the special power to encourage us toward more expressive and outwardly engaging moods.

Many spiritual paths encourage prayer, meditation, and spiritual activity at dawn to fully align ourselves to the energy of the day. Personally, the practice of early to bed and early to rise has always proven ridiculously challenging in my life and does not appear to vibe with my body's natural rhythm, at least for the time being. Every body is different, so it's good to either work with what is comfortable or try new experimental sleep/wake routines from time to time. It can be healthy to take a break from the routines that we find most comfortable, as this can encourage personal adaptability and fortitude through change.

This exercise assumes that you are awakening for the day, but readers who work the graveyard shift can modify the activities to suit their own purposes. This activity can be practiced and modified as frequently as you wish.

1. When you awaken for the day, whether naturally or by alarm, immediately bring your awareness to the fact that you are emerging from the dream world. You may wish to say to yourself, "I am awakening." Guide your mind's attention to the present moment. If you remember your dreams, this is a good opportunity to quickly jot notes about those experiences in your journal; you can reflect on these at a later time.

2. With a candle and lighter at your bedside, light the candle, sit up straight, and enter a calm, meditative state. It is easiest to meditate upon awakening. Bring your focus to your breath, having awareness of each inhalation and exhalation. Breathe deeply and find yourself connected to the reality in which you find yourself. Gently bring your focus to the candle flame, and contemplate what the existence of fire on earth means to us as a species. Fire and electricity heat our homes, our water, and our food and provide illumination when nighttime falls. Extend gratitude to the flame, the mysterious and enlightening force that it is, and extinguish the candle with one blow.

3. When you're ready, perform a few morning stretches. Don't make the bed right away. Head for the shower and attune yourself to the element of water as the water is washing over your body. Think about water's cleansing properties and how lucky we are to have access to hot, flowing water in our homes. Mentally express gratitude to the element of water as you cleanse yourself physically and spiritually, allowing the energy of dreaming to slip down the drain.

4. Unless it's a bitterly cold day, don't dry yourself off after the shower. Instead, go outside your home (cover yourself if you must!) and feel the sensation of air vaporizing the water droplets across your body. Take deep breaths and allow yourself to merge with the sensation, even if it's a bit uncomfortable at first. Face the sun and breathe in its gorgeous solar essence while you think about the sun's life-giving influence on the earth and her inhabitants. When your body feels dry and your thoughts feel positive, express gratitude both to the sun and to the element of air.

5. Next, grab your yoga mat or get situated on a comfortable floor space. Perform some yoga, both standing and seated, whether you're new to yogic practice or are a seasoned practitioner. Stretch in ways that feel right, holding each posture (*asana*) for at least fifteen seconds. No matter how simple or complex the poses are, moving the body can help to ground your energy into physical reality. Be sure to perform some postures that involve both your hands and your feet touching the ground. As you do so, take deep breaths and visualize the energy of Mother Earth entering your senses and surrounding your aura. When finished, extend gratitude to the element of earth.

6. Finally, when you find yourself ready to drink some coffee, tea, or juice, take slow slips of the beverage and visualize it nourishing your mind, body, and spirit. Think about ways in which the beverage was created by *all four elements*. Perform a similar contemplation with your breakfast, even if it's only a simple banana or a slice of toast. Extend gratitude to all of the elements while you slowly experience the food and drink that now begin the graceful merging process with your physical body.

7. As you go about your day, bring your attention to the four elements and consider how they all connect to the greatest element of all: spirit. Contemplate how the four terrestrial elements help maintain and sustain life on this planet and create a fertile environment for conscious life to take shape, grow, and evolve in. Journal your reflections in order to see how this practice affects you empathically and how your experience with this exercise changes with repeated practice.

chapter five

# Empathic Self-Care

Empaths are often the last people to ask for help from others. This is ironic because we are often the ones most in need of healing and care.

One reason why so many empaths are hesitant to accept care is because we don't wish to burden others with our problems or the darkness we may carry. This is an understandable dilemma, but please believe me when I say that healers of all varieties *love* sharing their gifts and abilities with people who are receptive and who genuinely benefit from them. As you may be aware with your own healing skills, it is a pleasurable and uplifting experience to help others feel better. It is fulfilling for healers to provide aid in whatever form their practice takes, even if it's only conversational support. You are meant to receive care because you are so talented at giving it to others yourself.

This chapter will examine ways in which we empaths can nurture ourselves and our gifts. Self-care is one of the most important things we can do. That's where it all begins.

## Receiving Care

Sometimes it's hard to recognize when we are in need of care. There are times when we are teetering between "everything's cool" and "everything's falling apart," and God knows we don't want to lean too far into the latter! When we don't feel secure in our lives, it's time to reach out. Odds are that you have friends and family who care about your wellbeing. If you feel this is not the case, recognize the fact that you *can* seek friendships and partnerships and that healing is always available in numerous forms.

Pursuing healing from others is not a sign of weakness. Quite the contrary; it's a sign of strength and self-awareness. Empaths are quite often catalysts for healing in others, so it's essential for us to allow ourselves to accept and enjoy uplifting energy from those who work in healing professions. When people shut themselves off from comfort from others, they are making the choice to exist fully in their mind. As you know, the mind plays tricks. We are all in this game of life together, and each of us has special skills, talents, and callings that are designed to help others on their journey. Even the most enlightened teacher knows when it's time to seek healing from outside sources; no one is entirely self-sufficient.

Empaths need external treatment sometimes. For some this is weekly, for others it's monthly, and for others it's yearly. It depends entirely on the person! When seeking help from others, it's essential to be totally honest with yourself and the practitioner. If you have reservations, concerns, or questions, make them known right from the start. Don't hold back because you are worried about offending the practitioner. Odds are that the practitioner will love to answer questions and create dialogue because it can increase confidence in both parties.

———————

*Pursuing healing from others is not a sign of weakness. Quite the contrary; it's a sign of strength and self-awareness. Empaths are quite often catalysts for healing in others, so it's essential for us to allow ourselves to accept and enjoy uplifting energy from those who work in healing professions.*

———⊙———

### *Everyday Empathic Techniques*

Here are a few of the many healing methods available that can be of great assistance to empaths. If money is a challenge in pursuing any of these practices, please be aware that many practitioners are open to working in trade or in small payment plans, and some are even covered by insurance. Many of these services are available free of charge and simply take a bit of research to locate.

For example, massage school students often need to work a certain number of volunteer hours to gain certification. Psychotherapy is often available from state-run healthcare facilities at very low prices or even free of charge. Numerous no-cost crisis lines and text lines exist to help those in need. It's easy for empaths to get discouraged when an easy option doesn't immediately present itself, so find the strength to recognize when you need some type of healing work and make the effort to make it happen. You can, you will, and you deserve it.

- **Massage:** I can't think of a better way for empaths to ground mental and emotional energy back into the physical body than to have someone give it a thorough rubdown! With the right massage therapist, we can cultivate a sense of safety and familiarity, even if we make an appointment only once or twice a year. Everyone has a different massage preference. Some like it light, while others prefer deep-tissue. Some prefer a particular gender for their massage therapist, while others have no preference. Massage can occur on a regular basis or simply as needed and is not a treatment limited to muscle strain or injury. The magic of human touch can be greatly healing on a spiritual and an emotional level.

- **Energy work:** Empaths, psychics, and other nontraditional spiritual folk are often fans of energy work. Many people are also familiar with the gift of hands-on healing that we all inherently possess. When healers fine-tune their energetic healing abilities, a world of possibilities opens for the practitioner and clients alike. Every energy worker is different, and many focus on a specialized area. Perhaps the most common style of energy healing is the art of Reiki, which was developed in Japan in 1922.

- **Acupuncture and Traditional Chinese Medicine:** Traditional Chinese Medicine (TCM) is becoming increasingly popular in the West and involves improving the flow of *chi*, or *ki* (the body's life force energy), throughout the system of meridians (energy channels) in the human body. The ancient herbal treatments utilized in TCM are perhaps the most physiologically based treatment methods and are similar to other forms of herbalism. As with all alternative healing modalities, it's important for any potential client to do their research and see what they feel called to pursue.

- **Shamanic journeying:** The word *shaman*—quite possibly the most overused term in alternative healing—was originally an anthropological term applied to particular ethnic tribes. It later became a widespread reference to practitioners of indigenous religious and magical practices, in particular those whose customs include spirit communication and inner-plane work, many of which utilize some amount of entheogens (mind-altering substances). Modern shamanic practice takes numerous forms, especially in the West, all of which draw on ancient practices and philosophies to one extent or another. Deeply transformative healing can occur, depending on the practitioner and the method utilized, and it's important for potential clients to research each practitioner's training background. Research is especially important because the title *shaman* has so often become an exploited badge of ego for some who claim its power. In other words, modern shamanic practice is a big hit-or-miss, so please be careful and discerning when choosing a practitioner to work with.

- **Divination:** Divinatory practices have been utilized in virtually all cultures around the world throughout the expanse of human history. In the modern Western world, one is most likely to encounter a plentiful number of tarot readers without venturing too far from home. Being a widespread modern practice, divination is seen as a method of gaining psychic insight by deciphering signs and synchronicities. Some of the most common divinatory tools include tarot cards, oracle cards, runes, tea leaf reading, bone/shell throwing, pendulums, and scrying implements (crystal balls, bowls of water, gemstones, and so on). Every psychic reader interprets their art differently, so it's wise to get a second or third opinion if at all possible.

## Empathic Sleep, Exercise, and Diet

Without a doubt, empaths are extremely sensitive to changes in diet, sleep, and daily routines. I can't overstate the importance of mindfulness when it comes to personal care. As the wise have always said, we can't meet the needs of others if we don't first take care of ourselves.

There is a time in every empath's life when we neglect our own wellbeing in order to focus on others. This is often borne of a feeling of responsibility coupled with personal depression, and can last anywhere from a brief period of time to a number of years. We can break through these detrimental patterns when we cultivate a greater sense of self-respect and learn the importance of self-care.

Part of this process is not only educating ourselves about the importance of physical health but also putting this knowledge into practice.

### Sleep

Ever since I can remember, I've been extremely sensitive to cycles of sleep. I feel lucky to have been raised in a family where getting a full night's sleep was seen as a valuable component of healthy functioning—although early morning schooldays threw a big ol' wrench in the works!

The idea of getting eight hours of sleep nightly has been tested time and time again; it is the median number of hours on which most people thrive healthfully. There are also plenty of folks who do well on less sleep. Others function best with a bit more sleep than average, while others have no problem sleeping in unconventional increments. It's all about finding your rhythm and experimenting to find what works best for you.

It's believed that most people function optimally by waking up at the same time every morning and that it's ideal to hit the hay at the same time every night. It's comforting to have a specific sleep pattern every day, but for many people in the world it's not always feasible. It's actually healthy to have a change in routine at times, as it makes us a bit more adaptable to change.

If you suffer from insomnia, you might consider trying various all-natural sleep supplements to see what works for you. In extremely difficult cases, it can be helpful for a physician to prescribe a pharmaceutical sleep aid. Sleep aids of all varieties can be of great benefit, but we don't want to become overly dependent on external herbs or chemicals. Under a doctor's or herbalist's care, we can experiment with lower doses and skipping doses if we feel a dependency developing.

Many empaths whom I've consulted with find themselves sleeping best with some white noise in the background, such as the noise generated by a fan, humidifier, or air purifier. Others prefer gentle sleepytime music, such as New Age tunes, piano, ambient electronica, and nature sounds. I've noticed that most of the people I know who prefer absolute silence during sleep tend to be more psychic in nature. This makes sense considering the mind of a psychic is often bombarded with external thoughts and spiritual communications! Whatever the case, everyone is different, and we must find what is most conducive to our own good night's sleep.

In addition to monitoring our sleep schedules and routines, it's very important to eliminate as much stress from our evening routines as possible. Getting a restful night's sleep can be a great challenge during times of high stress, so it does no good to be a nervous wreck before bedtime. In addition, stress and depression can sometimes make us want to sleep and sleep and sleep, regardless of our day's obligations. If you ever feel yourself sliding into this type of behavior, please seek help immediately to get back into a healthy routine. You deserve balance and wellbeing. We all do.

### Exercise

Our physical body is host to our mental, emotional, and spiritual bodies. Our fleshy vehicle deserves the utmost care, nourishment, and health. Exercising may not be the first thing that comes to mind when thinking about empathic self-care, but, much like massage therapy, physical exercise can help ground mental and emotional energy back into the body by way of concentrated movement. Many empaths find great benefit in following an instructional course or even working with a personal trainer. There is little room for slacking when there is a structured program to follow.

There are countless styles of exercise courses available in any given locale. It can also be fun to exercise privately in one's own home. I've found that following YouTube workout videos can be a joy! Personally, I'm a big fan of following along with various yoga video routines as well as practicing daily on my own and sometimes taking a weekly yoga class with a buddy. The art of yoga is a beloved practice for many emotionally sensitive souls, and if you are a typical water-loving empath, don't forget about swimming! I encourage you to find a routine that works for you and makes you feel good at the end of the day.

## *Diet*

Sometimes it's easy to forget how important our diet is for maintaining holistic health. We often witness the endorsement of dietary extremes in many countries. On the one hand, we find an abundance of fast-food joints and cheap, highly processed, unhealthy food in grocery stores, waiting to be consumed regardless of the consequences. On the other hand, we find extreme dietary trends and the cruel practice of "weight shaming" in everyday advertising. These extremes of dietary encouragement can leave us feeling confused and unconfident, which often leads to dietary apathy.

Empaths and other sensitive individuals are highly susceptible to the effects of our dietary routines. Everything we consume and experience in life has a direct link to our emotional state at any given time. We are presented with the challenge of seeing through financial corporate greed, especially in the realm of food consumption. Issues surrounding global food production and distribution are a *huge* can of worms that is probably best not opened here and now. However, please feel free to check out the sections on diet, green living, and sustainability in my previous book *Esoteric Empathy*.

For our purposes, suffice it to say that we empaths *must* cultivate dietary consciousness in order to stay healthy on every level. Our relationship to food constitutes our relationship to the earth. The food and drink we consume can be considered a sacrament of Mother Earth. When we fall into the trap of simply consuming "whatever" for the sake of convenience, we are disrespecting both the earth and ourselves. But it's a process. No one's perfect.

Then again, it's equally unwise to be an obsessive health nut! I have witnessed many people engage in an extreme dietary routine coupled with a divisive sense of self-righteousness. I did this for years myself. In reality, any extreme is unhealthy; balance is the key. We can't beat ourselves up if we have a craving for french fries now and then. At the end of the day, we need to listen to what our body is communicating.

If you consume a lot of processed foods throughout the day, become aware of how your body responds to them. Do you feel sluggish, bloated, or sweaty? Is your digestive system functioning irregularly? These physical signs are easy for empaths to dismiss, especially for those of us who aren't always grounded in our body. Just the same, take note of how you feel after consuming fresh, vibrant, organic, local, and minimally processed foods. Not only do these foods taste better and carry more of Mama Nature's energy, but they also tend to support small-scale agriculture and ethical economies.

Let's talk about meat for a minute. The consumption of animal flesh continues to be a hot-button ethical debate, especially for people like us who demonstrate a deeper connection to emotions and conscious living. Humans are omnivorous, meaning that we can consume both flora and fauna. Our teeth and digestive system have the capacity to engage in meat eating or not. Our ancestors survived largely on meat, especially those in colder climates. For eons of human history, meat has been hunted, fished, and raised for consumption. But there's one really big difference: these forms of ethical and nature-based meat consumption are *drastically* different from the practices of the modern meat industry.

I can think of few industries that are as horrific and torturous as "factory farming." Divorced from the cycle of nature, these industries are focused on the bottom dollar, not on giving animals healthy or happy lives. These large-scale industries often raise animals in crowded conditions (usually in piles of their own filth) and give them chemical-laden feed. Most mass-produced chickens, pigs, and cows never see the light of day or feel the touch of grass beneath their feet. These industries are truly torturous, and I urge every reader to research the horrors of large-scale meat production. Why would we want to promote industries like these, and why would we as empaths wish to invite such emotional suffering into our sphere? We simply cannot afford to hide the truth behind closed doors.

In general, meat consumption seems to be more natural and sustainable in colder climates, whereas many warmer locations closer to the equator have full-year growing cycles of fruits and vegetables. In these places, vegetarianism, veganism, and rarely-consuming-meat-ism are often reasonable choices. For empaths across the world, the choice of whether or not to consume meat is a big one and is not always black-or-white. Although supermarkets and restaurants don't always offer ethical alternatives, we ourselves have the option of buying meat, dairy products, and eggs from local farmers and smaller "humanely raised" producers. This includes products from grocery stores that specialize in healthier, more sustainable, and ethically sourced products, as well as smaller restaurants that locally source their food. These options don't always break the bank, either. In fact, a lot of ethically produced and local food is comparable in price to the food produced by larger industries. We just need to find out where to look.

Luckily, more and more food producers are becoming wise to the fact that people care about their health, care about the environment, and care about animals. Our dollars are like votes, and when we give our cash to well-deserving and progressive food producers, we literally help steer the world in a better direction while simultaneously enriching our body, mind, and spirit.

## Working with Anxiety and Depression

All right, this is a big one. Empaths the world over are prone to suffer from anxiety and depression on a regular basis—or at least in recurring cycles. We have a tendency to carry both our own emotional weight and that of outside forces. We feel things very deeply, and this can contribute to ongoing anxiety, depression, and emotional imbalance.

There really is no easy answer to managing these feelings; there is no cure-all. But there is a *lot* we can do to work with these feelings and find our balance. If we think that it's impossible to heal and that we are doomed to an empathic state of darkness, those beliefs can easily become self-fulfilling prophecies. We have to start by being our own advocate. We must realize that our emotional wellness is no one's responsibility but our own. We must have the self-respect to take matters into our own hands. We must cultivate empathy for ourselves. Every problem has a solution, so let's strive not to give in to pessimism and hopelessness. Let's find the resources we need to heal emotionally. It's never too late.

## Negative Imprints

Words can never hurt me? Yeah, right! Those of us who are emotionally sensitive can hold on to verbally abusive criticism for years. When external critiques become internalized, we can't help but wonder if they're true. Empaths are notorious for overthinking things. Sometimes criticism is constructive, but other times it's destructive. It's imperative that we differentiate between the two. It's important for us to examine different styles of communication and figure out where any given person is coming from. Is it from a place of division or a place of love? Empaths need to meditate, focus, and examine criticism in any given moment, including any critiques from the past that we are still holding on to.

When empaths unconsciously carry guilt, shame, and harsh self-judgment, these patterns of belief can leave us feeling embittered and jaded over time. In fact, these feelings in excess can chip away at our compassion, making us more emotionally distant and reclusive. This is not what it means to activate our gifts. Empathy is an amazing and evolutionary gift, not a curse!

Even the smallest negative occurrence can affect empaths, so we need to take humble steps toward activating the self-awareness required to heal potentially negative imprints. As an example, a number of years ago I went on a pilgrimage to the gorgeous Sri Ganesha Hindu Temple in Utah with some of my spiritual comrades. We regularly visit this temple and have forged a beautiful bond between our own small temple and this beautiful facility. During this visitation, we went out to eat at a local Indian restaurant after spending time at the temple. I didn't have enough cash on me at the time to leave more than a 10 percent tip for the servers and staff. Over the following week, my mind kept going back to that experience, wishing that I had been able to leave a more suitable tip. So, upon payday, I mailed them a nice, crisp twenty dollar bill with a letter of gratitude for the restaurant's healthful selections and compassionate service. This simple act instantly helped me feel like I had corrected a mistake by returning their kindness. A little creative action can truly go a long way!

---

*Words can never hurt me? Yeah, right! Those of us who are emotionally sensitive can hold on to verbally abusive criticism for years. When external critiques become internalized, we can't help but wonder if they're true. Empaths are notorious for overthinking things. Sometimes criticism is constructive, but other times it's destructive. It's imperative that we differentiate between the two.*

### Therapy

When it comes to empathic healing, I cannot overstate the importance of counseling. Whether we choose psychotherapy, psychiatry, cognitive behavioral therapy, life coaching, or any other approach, empaths *need* to have someone to talk to sometimes. For those who have long-lasting emotional traumas, regular counseling can be profoundly beneficial in the healing process. Some empaths do best with regular counseling, while others do well with as-needed sessions. Some of us also require herbal or pharmaceutical medication in addition to the counsel of a professional with whom we can share ideas and perspectives.

It takes some degree of humility to seek help from outside sources, especially when it comes to something as sensitive and vulnerable as our darker emotions and traumas. But remember, these people are professionally *trained* in this work. It's also reassuring to know that empathic therapeutic approaches are now becoming recognized as invaluable assets to the healing process.

## Social Media

I've gotta say it: if you're a frequent user of social media, please consider taking a break from it from time to time. It's essential for us empaths to disconnect and unplug sometimes so we can totally focus on our own wellbeing. Viewing social-media updates can inundate our senses with a large amount of information in a very small amount of time. It's easy to get empathically overloaded from viewing emotional photos and posts. Remember, we don't consume only food; all of our interactions, whether in person or remotely, are also a form of energetic consumption and emotional engagement. Everything we view, experience, and think about has an effect on our empathy to some degree.

## Environment

Our environment has an effect on our empathy as well, most importantly our home environment and our workplace. If these environments make us feel uncomfortable or otherwise imbalanced, we *must* work for change, even if it seems like change in these situations is unattainable. There's always something that can be done to improve our level of comfort in any situation: someone can be talked to, goals can be set, and boundaries can be made known.

## Everyday Empathic Techniques

Here are a few techniques that can be helpful when dealing with anxiety and depression. Please add to this list and discover what works best for you. Most importantly, don't give in to those overwhelming feelings of hopelessness. Everything happens for a reason, and it's our responsibility to learn life's lessons, no matter how difficult. We must find our way out of the darkness, which can seem so heavy. We must, we can, and we will.

- **Mental focus:** When your emotions are overwhelming, get yourself in a safe space, slow your breathing, and focus on the issue. Remember that these feelings are subject to change; everything will pass in time. Knowing that you are safe, try looking at your feelings from a rational, cognitive standpoint. Choose to loosen your attachment to the emotions by bringing them to the problem-solving mind.

- **Breathing:** When we are overcome with anxiety, we may instinctively practice shallow or rapid breathing. Try not to do this! Bring attention to your breath in the moment, ensuring that you take nice, long, deep breaths from the diaphragm, ideally in through the nose and out of the mouth.

- **Invoke humor:** Laughter is good medicine. If there is any way you can incorporate humor or lightheartedness into a depressive or anxious situation, it can go a long way in lifting your mood. Empaths are notorious for taking things too seriously, and sometimes it's just not worth it. Sometimes challenges are easier to solve than they appear, and injecting a bit of cheerfulness into a situation is a great way to lighten the gravity of it.

- **Constructive conversation:** Rather than believing that it's you against the world, talk to someone! Get a new perspective. Share your feelings and allow someone else to share; it feels good for both parties. Whether it's a friend, a family member, or even a total stranger from a crisis helpline, people do care about you and are happy to lend a hand, a shoulder, or an ear. You are never alone.

- **Activity:** As we have discussed, various activities can help the overwhelmed empath, including exercise, yoga, art, relaxing music, meditation, bathing, massage, aromatherapy, pets, self-pampering, taking personal space, achieving restful sleep, and so many more.

- **Medicinal support:** There are many all-natural supplements, herbs, tinctures, and medicines that are designed to help alleviate depression and anxiety. Everyone responds differently to different things, so it's worth experimenting carefully with various over-the-counter products on the market, assuming they do not negatively interact with any other medications you may be taking. Personally, I have found great success using the Bach flower essence called Rescue Remedy. My body also responds well to valerian and kava supplements. Additionally, during times of high stress, I will take my prescribed Propranolol, a light beta blocker that successfully stops symptoms of panic attack and has very few known risks or side effects.

- **Perspective:** It's ridiculously easy to get lost in our thoughts, missing the forest for the trees. When we become overly self-focused, we lose track of the bigger picture. When we obsess about the details of temporary roadblocks, we truly are making emotional mountains out of molehills. We are stronger than we believe. Don't lose perspective. Look around you and count your blessings. Look at the amazing and innovative technologies around us. Look at what we take for granted every day. Despite life's challenges, we are so very fortunate. Gratitude can inspire profound life changes and create genuine happiness.

- **Contact a helpline:** If you are feeling extremely depressed, anxious, or suicidal, talk to a professional who wants to help you and is trained to do so. If immediate in-person counseling is unavailable, contact your local hospital (or call 911) and ask for the mental health department. Alternatively, if you live in the Unites States, you can call the National Suicide Prevention Lifeline at 1-800-273-8255. Or if it's more comfortable for you, you can send a text message to a compassionate volunteer crisis counselor at the Crisis Text Line by texting 741741. These wonderful services are freely available twenty-four hours a day. Similar helpful services exist internationally if you live outside the US.

### *Exercise:* Overloaded: A Bathtime Cleansing

Most empaths have an affinity for water. As an element, water is known across mystical systems for being aligned with emotions, intuition, and empathy. Water cleanses us emotionally and energetically while also removing dirt and grime from our bodies. Cleanliness is next to godliness, right?

It's nice to take a shower and cleanse off for the day or evening, but there's a certain magic about the bathtub. Baths are intimate and private. Instead of being surrounded by rushing, fast-paced water, the bathtub provides a vessel in which we can lie back, unwind, relax, and calmly cleanse ourselves on many levels.

This empathic cleansing exercise makes use of the bathtub. If you don't have one, you may wish to ask to use the tub of a friend or family member, or seek out a private hot spring in your area, or even use a jacuzzi if you have access to one.

As always, feel free to modify this exercise to suit your needs and preferences. Be sure to journal your experience with this and other empathic cleansing exercises and reflect on the effects for future reference.

1. Perform any necessary preparations for your bath. Prep your space in whatever way works best for you: dim the lights, light a candle or some soothing incense, put on some relaxing music, pour a glass of wine, or add some bath salts or essential oils.

2. Once the bath is drawn, ensure that the temperature is hot but not scalding. Test the water with your hands and feet and modify the temperature as needed so that when you submerge yourself, you will feel an instant sense of relaxation. After you have done so, slow your breathing and make sure that every part of your body gets wet.

3. Attune yourself to the spirit of the water. It should feel gentle, calm, and relaxing. Close your eyes and imagine the water as a single drop within the vast expanse of the world's rivers, lakes, and oceans. See yourself floating in this droplet, suspended in embryonic bliss. Reconnect to your innocent and childlike self by releasing any judgments that pop into your head. Simply exist.

4. When ready, open your eyes and envision the water glowing in various shades of blue and green, and any other colors you associate with the water element. Put your hands palms up on the water's surface while envisioning these colors rising out of the tub and surrounding your body. Slowly breathe in this energy, allowing it to gently permeate your body inside and out.

5. See this watery energy form a sphere around your head, and allow your thoughts to be cleansed. Visualize this energy slowly expanding to encompass your throat, cleansing your speech and actions. See the energy meeting your arms and hands, blessing your good work in the world. At your heart, the energy purifies your emotions and reminds you to live with love. At your belly area, the watery energy cleanses your sense of confidence and social support. At the genital region, the energy cleanses your sexuality and your physical health. Upon visualizing the energy washing over your legs and feet, affirm that your path in life is guided by empathy through and through.

6. Visualize this wave of empathic energy expanding far beyond you, growing beyond the room, beyond the house, beyond your city, beyond your country, and beyond our planet, and bursting out in a wave across the expanse of the universe.

7. Open your eyes and give yourself time to come back to your body. Perform some more deep breathing and conclude with any affirmations, prayers, or statements that have significance to you personally. Verbally give thanks to the

element of water. Let the water fully drain before you exit the tub. In the meantime, visualize the water element washing away the last bit of your stress so you feel fully rejuvenated and ready to face whatever life has to offer.

chapter six

# Empathic Expression

We empaths have a huge well of emotions inside us that need to be expressed in some manner. I talked earlier about the absorptive and projective aspects of the empathic experience. One of the major ways we can process emotions is to express them, whether this means talking to someone, performing self-healing techniques, or creating expressive art.

The neat thing about art is that, in reality, it is limitless. There are no boundaries to artistic expression. Just take this book, for example. Personally, I consider this book and my previous books to be pieces of art. Additionally, the cover of the book and its layout are also works of art designed to convey the book's intellectual and emotional content.

Everywhere you look, there is art! In everything from the cinematography of a TV show to the details of a sculpture, the artistic spirit is making itself known. Any heartfelt expression can be considered art, even something as simple as a well-crafted letter to a friend. Expression in any form helps empaths process their emotions and initiate the healing process for themselves and others.

## Spiritual Art

Many artists who are metaphysically inclined tend to believe that we either consciously or subconsciously communicate with spirits, astral guides, and our higher self when channeling artistic work. Some also believe that artistic inspiration is drawn from the akashic records, an astral storehouse of information documenting the whole of human experience, including past lives, the present life, and even future lifetimes.

Spiritual artists create intentionally channeled pieces such as those produced through automatic drawing, automatic writing, and automatic vocalism. These channelings are typically produced with the artist in a trancelike state, in which they act as a spiritual filter for external (or internal) communications. In most cases, these mystics produce work that feels distinct from their own personality, especially because they don't usually remember creating the pieces that they've channeled during meditation. This type of channeling can be challenging for strong empaths because we naturally have a fear of being overtaken by external energy.

Due to a fear of energetic invasion and a tendency toward self-criticism and overthinking, many empaths face difficulty in permitting their artistic side to flourish. I feel that empaths in particular could do well with a burst of self-assurance when it comes to artistic creation. Most empaths are natural artists. Due to social conditioning, we have a tendency to second-guess ourselves expressively. This self-criticism manifests most often in conversational exchanges because we have a desire for everyone to get along. At times it feels like our own personal opinions and viewpoints are overshadowed by those of others. In many cases, this is because we allow it to occur. Too many empathic souls have become accustomed to letting other people dictate their lives, their very beliefs. It seems easier that way. It takes less effort. But emotional submission can be both inauthentic and danger-ous. It's noble for empaths to hold steadfast to their viewpoints and to express themselves in any creative form.

———————

*Too many empathic souls have become accustomed to letting other people dictate their lives, their very beliefs. It seems easier that way. It takes less effort. But emotional submission can be both inauthentic and dangerous. It's noble for empaths to hold steadfast to their viewpoints and to express themselves in any creative form.*

*Artistic Therapy*

Therapeutic approaches to art have become commonplace in schools, hospitals, rehabilitation centers, and numerous other fa-cilities. Sometimes all it takes for a person to tap into their artistic potential is some prompting from another person. If this is the case for you, please allow my own prompting to jump-start your process!

Art therapy gives people a chance to express their feelings and channel them into something meaningful, even if the individuals are not particularly skilled in the mediums. In reality, artistic skill is irrelevant: everyone has the capability to craft pieces of work that are creative and transformative. Art is alchemy.

The reason why artistic expression can be so therapeutic is because it allows us to put our feelings into form. Even if the form is nonphysical (musical art, for example), we are given the opportunity to take emotional energy out of ourselves and put it into a tangible form in a cathartic act of healing—even if we choose not to share our creation with other people. Again, there are no hard-and-fast rules when it comes to artistic expression. Why is this? Because *everything* is art!

## Creative Self-Image and Inspiration

Empaths are acutely tapped into the emotions of themselves and others. I would argue that empaths *must* make art in some form in order to stay healthy and happy. Although big galleries and highfalutin artists might make us think that "the arts" are exclusive domains of only the most talented, the truth is that everyone has an artist inside them and *every* work of art is valuable in its own way. We don't need to be perfect. Perfection is an illusion.

I remember writing loads of dark, Gothic poetry throughout high school. Looking back, these pieces of poetry now seem cheesy and melodramatic, but it was helpful for me to create them during that time in my life. I don't share those pieces with anyone these days, admittedly in part because of negative criticism I received from those who were more educated in classic poetry. But that's okay. Those pieces were like prayers or spells woven during that time in my life; they were therapeutically beneficial. I also had an affinity for mystical black-and-white photography throughout high school, and although I would not necessarily create such abstract pieces at this point in my life, the expression helped me externalize my empathy and my individuality at the time. I wouldn't take these expressions back for anything in the world, even though I see them in a different light now.

Similarly, as a little kid, I costarred in numerous local plays, having the time of my life memorizing lines, songs, and dance moves and dressing up like fantastical characters. I remember wanting to carry on with these performances in high school, so I tried out for my first play during my freshman year as part of an after-school program. Unbeknownst to me, it was a *musical*. During the audition, I expressed to the drama teacher that I didn't feel comfortable trying to sing; I didn't know how to sing. The teacher held up my theater application, ripped the paper in two, and declared in front of everyone, "Then you will *not* be considered!" I was emotionally affected by this exchange, choosing to leave the theater, cry for a good while, and never audition for another performance. This experience was bittersweet because on one hand, I allowed it to derail my relationship with the performing arts. On the other hand, it helped shift my life's focus to other expressions to which I am better suited—writing books, for example!

We empaths tend to be notoriously self-critical and harsh on ourselves. Sometimes we become utterly obsessive about our mistakes and regrets. This mentality doesn't help our energy move along; it keeps us stuck in a lower frequency of imbalance and pain. We can make a choice to actively and humbly seek resolution for errors of the past rather than remain trapped in a vicious cycle of shame. Although it can be easy to feel guilty and engage in harsh self-judgment, this really does a disservice to everyone. We can uplift and inspire others when we model this behavior ourselves.

It's beneficial for us empaths to immerse ourselves in a variety of artistic expressions in order to discover what we vibe with. We can't be good at everything, but sometimes we can find those niches where we feel naturally talented. When we feel confident in our expressions, we can really start rockin' our skills on a regular basis and fine-tune our abilities.

As I've mentioned, we need to stop being so critical of ourselves. Even if we fear judgment from others, there's no sense in adopting a self-defeating mentality. We can't let fear guide our every movement. There's no way to please everyone in life, and there will always be someone who is better than us at any given thing. But it's really not a competition. Besides, we don't even need to share our art with other people if we don't feel comfortable doing so. The most important thing is to express ourselves, even if we aren't always pleased with the results. By experimenting with different mediums, including mixed media, we can discover our own unique callings and expressive talents. When we choose not to exercise self-judgment, we can more easily break through barriers that keep us from trying in the first place.

Personally, if I don't like a piece of visual art I've created, I stick it in the "burning box" at the nonprofit multicultural temple that I co-operate. Every Halloween, we burn the items in this box as a way to release the energy to the universe. Also included in this box are old drafts, old paperwork, and of course old bills! We call it the "spiritual shredder." So if you feel uncomfortable with a piece of art you have created, you may consider safely burning it outside, thereby releasing its energy to the flow of the universe. This is especially relevant if you have created a piece that is aimed at transforming personal trauma or negative imprints from the past. On the flip side, it can be equally beneficial to burn pieces that are themselves prayers for yourself, others, or the world at large. For example, a large sketch symbolizing world peace would be ideal to burn on a sunny day in order to help metaphysically send its energy out into the world. Along similar lines, some people I know prefer to burn their old vision board, which is a constructive form of art that I will explore in the next chapter.

———————

*We empaths tend to be notoriously self-critical and harsh on ourselves. Sometimes we become utterly obsessive about our mistakes and regrets. This mentality doesn't help our energy move along; it keeps us stuck in a lower frequency of imbalance and pain. We can make a choice to actively and humbly seek resolution for errors of the past rather than remain trapped in a vicious cycle of shame.*

## Creative Muses and Guides

Artists love their muses. In Greek mythology, the Muses are the nine daughters of Zeus and Mnemosyne. They were often prayed to in ancient Greece and Rome for assistance with creative endeavors, with each Muse overseeing a particular form of artistic expression. The ancient Greek poet Hesiod regularly invoked the Muses when crafting his art.

The nine creative Muses are there for all of us to commune with at any time! My favorite musical artist, empathic songstress Tori Amos, frequently makes mention of the Muses and various spirits that visit her when channeling emotive pieces of music. Many artists of all varieties recognize the power of the Muses, whether actual or symbolic, in assisting with their creative endeavors.

One often hears mention of fellow humans who act as muses in a person's creative life. Perhaps one of the most famous examples was Ingrid Bergman, Alfred Hitchcock's muse. Another is Uma Thurman, muse to filmmaker Quentin Tarantino and the star of several of his films. Although Tarantino's films can be a bit too violent for the everyday empath, his connection with Ms. Thurman is one of great karmic synchronicity. When two people find themselves connected in inexplicable ways, any sort of creative collaboration can lead to dynamic results.

Whether artists work with human muses or the spiritual Muses, a certain energetic bond is forged between the creator and the inspirer. In many ways, *all* art is a collaborative effort. Even if an artist feels as if their work was entirely internally inspired, it's reasonable to imagine that some sort of connection was formed with other planes of reality. If an artist creates a particularly dark piece of expressive work, there is some sort of connection occurring between the conscious self and the unconscious plane. Just the same, angels or spirit guides may play some part in inspiring a particularly motivational piece of work that influences others toward a higher conscious understanding.

If you feel called to invite the powerful Muses into your artistic life, their specific rulerships are as follows. Simply speaking the name of a Muse and meditating on her qualities can forge a bond and invoke a very special creative vibration.

**Calliope**—Epic poetry

**Clio**—History

**Erato**—Erotic and choral poetry

**Euterpe**—Music and song

**Melpomene**—Tragedy and performance art

**Polyhymnia**—Hymns, religious poetry, and miming

**Terpsichore**—Light verse and dance

**Thalia**—Comedy and epic poetry

**Urania**—Astronomy and astrology

### *Exercise:* An Empathic Journey into Art

The purpose of this exercise is to immerse yourself in various forms of art at your own comfort level. If you choose to follow through with this empathic exercise, you may feel inclined to immerse yourself in only those artistic expressions that you are familiar with or have experimented with in the past. While this is beneficial, I recommend pushing your limits a bit and exploring artistic expressions that you may not feel immediately comfortable with. It may feel awkward at first, but it can be fun to *try*. Experimentation is deeply valuable for empathic souls because it can encourage us to try things that are unconventional or that we may have otherwise avoided.

It can be extremely healthy to push your limits a bit and put yourself out there. I remember a time a number of years ago when I felt greatly inspired by independent performance art. Upon watching various documentaries and surfing videos on YouTube for days on end, I witnessed abstract, haunting, and socially poignant performance pieces crafted and performed by brave individuals expressing themselves in unconventional ways. After fine-tuning a performance piece of my own, I scheduled times downtown to perform the silent piece for some very confused onlookers. This experience greatly pushed my limits of comfort but was beneficial in many ways. I could take this experience to a place of embarrassment—especially because of various criticisms I received—but it was personally meaningful at the time, and hopefully to others as well!

Some of the examples that follow do not necessarily involve you as the creator but rather as the viewer. With many forms of expression, it can be of great benefit to observe those who are experienced in any given field. We can gain inspiration by observing art that is intended for public enjoyment.

If you don't have a journal or diary already, I highly recommend beginning one. This exercise is a great opportunity to begin a journal—or dust off that old one you've been neglecting!

In addition to giving us the opportunity to express our thoughts and feelings, journaling helps us examine our experiences. It can be fascinating to reflect on journal entries many years down the road—don't even get me started on how crazy my journals are from twenty years ago! It can be fascinating to see how we develop intellectually and emotionally. When journaling, we can put our thoughts into form, similar to how we express ourselves in other creative arts.

When you immerse yourself in any of the arts that follow, be honest when describing your experiences. Note the pros and cons. What did you especially enjoy during the process of creating various pieces or observing others' creations? Would you be interested in researching the history of the artistic skill you are experiencing and/or creating? Do you feel like involving yourself further in any particular expression, perhaps taking a class or practicing at home on your own? These are potential ideas to note in your journal while exploring any of the expressions found here.

Most importantly, take note of how the art you experience affects you empathetically. Which emotions are evoked in you when experiencing different pieces of art? Do you believe that you are experiencing emotions that the artist intended you to experience? Could you be "empathing" emotions that the artist was feeling when creating the piece?

Keep in mind that it's good to experience a wide variety of art, regardless of the form, because it helps us remain curious and open to the wide array of creative expressions that the world has to offer.

I certainly don't list *every* potential artistic avenue here, so get creative! Try expanding this list and see where your own synchronistic life experiences guide you. Have fun!

- **Visual art:** Visual arts take so many forms that it would be impossible to list them all here. Perhaps the best thing for someone curious about expanding their knowledge of visual mediums would be to visit galleries. Art galleries generally specialize in visual art. Over the next few months, make plans to visit different galleries in your area. When you research local galleries, you may find that particular art installations stand out to you. There may be certain subjects that pique your interest, or you may be drawn to specific mediums, such as paintings, sketches, photography, found object pieces, mixed media work, or sculpted art. Plan to visit interesting local showings on opening night or possibly later on when not as many people will be present. You may even consider getting in touch with an artist if their work really speaks to you. (I've done this before, and it can give them a huge boost of confidence!) In your journal, take note of which styles of art affect you the most emotionally. You may find yourself giving serious consideration to trying some of these expressions on your own or signing up for local community art classes. Hey, why not?

- **Performance art:** Some of the oldest forms of expression, the theatrical arts take many forms and fulfill many social purposes. There are numerous types of theatrical performance, so when you explore this expressive avenue, it may be a good idea to explore a variety of performances in your community. As a member of an audience, you not only are lending support to artists and venues but are also being gifted a treat of living art that is the culmination of extensive planning and rehearsal. As part of your personal exploration, you may wish to attend a variety of performances, including but not limited to operas, plays, ballets, acrobatics, shadow puppetry, magic shows, drag shows, exotic dancing, live painting, and even street performances. If you feel drawn to the performing arts, make a list in your journal of your impressions of different styles and your personal experiences with them. What do you feel were the creative intentions behind the performances, and how did each style or piece affect you empathically?

- **Musical art:** Empaths are often mega fans of music because the expression is so palpable and direct. Music can be listened to at virtually any time, whether experienced attentively or while driving, cooking, cleaning, studying, relaxing, or anything else. Different music hits us in different ways, so it's important to know how different musical genres, instruments, vocals, and artists create an empathic link. In most cases, emotionally driven musical expressions can have a profound effect on our mood and our energetic vibration. As part of this exercise, I encourage you to experience different styles of music in various ways. For example, spend a few hours on the internet listening to genres and subgenres of music that you normally would not. How do these pieces affect your state of mind? Can you feel where the artist was coming from emotionally? You may also consider picking a few days to attend different live shows. It can be quite the experience to attend a singing bowl sound bath followed by a raucous punk rock show! Be sure to note your experiences in your journal and reflect on the possibility of learning to play an instrument or learning to sing yourself—or dusting off that old instrument from middle school band class!

- **Body practice:** While the performing arts certainly make use of the human body as a medium, there are plenty of physically creative pursuits that don't necessarily emphasize a performance aspect. Physical practices that blend spiritual and energetic principles can be deeply rewarding for empathic and otherwise sensitive souls. Yoga and meditation are perhaps two of the most valuable empathic tools. If you are relatively unfamiliar with these practices, I encourage you to register for local introductory classes and to explore instructive videos to practice on your own. Additional time-tested global practices that integrate physical and spiritual wellness include qigong, tai chi, and other martial arts. Also falling in this category of body art, dancing is a highly energizing form of expression. You may consider signing up for a local beginner-level class in African dance, salsa, swing, ballroom, ballet, hip-hop, or even something as unique as tap dancing! Many cities also offer freeform ecstatic dance gatherings, where attendees dance or meditate in their own freeform style while energizing music plays as a conduit for the experience.

- **Written art:** Creative expression by way of writing has been around since language was developed. In some styles of expression, more creative specifics can be conveyed through the written word than in some other creative mediums. Writing is intellectually engaging, often requiring an investment of time and attention. You can experiment with writing by considering different styles of this creative art. At the moment, for example, you are immersing yourself in a creative piece of nonfiction—the very book you hold in your hands! You are likely familiar with modern and classic novels, short stories, and other works of fiction, and each of these styles carries a different energy. You may consider reading various newspapers, magazines, and almanacs in order to get a feel for articles and pieces of journalism. I also recommend researching various types of blogs, whether written by your favorite celebrity or by individuals who are looking to make a positive social impact. You may also wish to brush up on some classic and modern poetry! Use your own written creativity to record notes in your journal, noting which particular styles of writing seem to speak the most to you as an empath. From there, contemplate the ways in which your own emotional energies could be expressed through the written word.

• **Edible art:** With one look at the incredible attention to detail put into fancy food presentations, one can witness the magic and art of food! A number of modern television shows are focused on the art of fine food. Quality foods of all types are nourishing on both the physical and the emotional level, which is why "foodcraft" can be so valuable for empaths. This is especially the case if organic, fair-trade, humane, and sustainable products are used in the preparation. Artistic food preparation doesn't have to be expensive. Do you know how many beautiful pieces can be made using mac 'n' cheese with a couple of sides? Have fun experimenting, and consider signing up for a cooking or baking class. Also keep in mind that a great many cooking tutorials are available in books and magazines and online. Use your journal to make notes of which foods are most appealing to you and why. If you were to pursue a craft of delectable edibles, which entrees, appetizers, snacks, or desserts do you feel would be most relaxing and enjoyable to work with? Finally, what are your thoughts about pursuing a deeper involvement in the art of gardening, farming, or other earth-based agricultural skills? Would you consider getting involved in a local small-scale farming community or sustainable food co-op? There are endless possibilities when exploring creative food production, preparation, and presentation. Just please save me some of that curry.

- **Old World art:** In addition to the agricultural arts we just discussed, there are endless options to explore in terms of Old World art. There is truly something magical about handmade, handpicked, and otherwise handcrafted items, to which mass factory-produced products simply cannot compare. When personal time, energy, and skill are put into creative pieces, a direct energetic and even empathic connection can be made between the creator and the experiencer. Various types of Old World arts include woodworking, metalworking, carpentry, needlework, beading, crochet, basket weaving, candle making, soap making, beekeeping, brewing, primitive survival skills, and so much more. Even the arts of herbalism and natural healing can fall in this category—anything from creating simple teas and tinctures to pursuing full-on training in Ayurvedic, Native American, Chinese, or Western herbal medicine. Note in your journal which Old World skills you are interested in experimenting with, and research classes in your area. As an empathic soul, which expressions do you feel are best suited to your own unique emotional nature?

chapter seven

# Spiritualizing Your Empathy

When a person begins studying the ins and outs of empathy, they are likely to discover very specific takes on the subject in theory and practice. When we study empathy within scientific fields such as biochemistry and psychotherapy, we see it in a strictly biological light. When we study empathy in metaphysical circles, we see it portrayed as a spiritual gift or ability, oftentimes with little mention of its legitimate scientific basis.

During the sixteenth century in Western culture, science and spirituality began to split into distinct entities. Over time, this division gave rise to the thinking that the two were mutually exclusive. A far-fetched idea formed that scientific fields were strictly divorced from metaphysics and that spiritual beliefs had little scientific basis. This split, however, did not occur as prominently in the East, as most of these cultures have always recognized the interconnectedness of physical existence and the metaphysical realms of reality.

Science and spirituality are two sides of the same coin; each has both great wisdom and blind spots. Neither science nor spirituality can be neglected when formulating a full picture of the universe or anything in it, including empathy.

Numerous spiritual traditions recognize that spirituality is part of everything in existence—everything! There is nothing that is not spiritual. In many ways, science and spirituality are complementary fields that communicate observations and theories about reality in different ways—simply from different vantage points.

We can intentionally incorporate a spiritual element into our everyday empathic existence. This will help us remain aware of the fact that empathic abilities have a more important place in the world than it may seem at times. Indeed, all acts of empathy are themselves spiritually significant, so it's important for us to keep ourselves balanced and aligned with these energies on a daily basis.

## Daily Prayer and Meditation

Regardless of how well we comprehend what empathy is on an intellectual level, the most important thing is that we actively work to maintain and balance our empathetic capabilities on a daily basis. Although some people choose to merely exist, life is an adventure worth actually living—and living well. Mystics worldwide have long understood the importance of daily spiritual practice. Eastern traditions recognize the yogic principle of *sadhana* as the process of utilizing our personal experiences for the greater spiritual good. This is most often understood in the context of daily intentional routines designed to keep us energetically aligned. Much as everybody's karma is unique, so is everybody's sadhana.

As we grow in awareness about what our empathetic gifts are and how they function, we find that we need some sort of grounding outlet to channel the abundance of energies we receive every day—not to mention our own internal energy.

Whether we are an empath or not, some type of daily prayer routine can be incredibly beneficial in keeping us connected to energies much greater than ourselves. Our own spiritual beliefs are irrelevant when it comes to daily prayer; even strict atheists can benefit from connecting to nature, calming the mind, and performing meditative exercises. What some folks deem spiritual, others see as merely psychological, and that's okay! Everyone has the capability to form a daily routine that fits their own constitution and callings.

If you are drawn to certain spiritual practices, consider ways in which you can devote yourself to your God, gods, gurus, angels, spiritual guides, or whomever you feel a direct connection with. Create a daily practice that allows you to empathetically share love with the divine and yourself. This can be accomplished in the morning or evening, or whenever it suits your fancy. Individualization, modification, and steadfast dedication are all marks of successful devotion.

### Creating a Routine

Spiritual routines can be both mentally and emotionally grounding. Personally, I devote the first part of every morning—even if I'm in a rush to get to an appointment—to performing certain prayers, mantras, and devotions to certain deities and spirits with whom I feel a great spiritual connection. No matter how pressing my morning schedule, I always perform some amount of yoga in order to align my body and mind to the daily cycle. I make it a point to draw energy from the sun and the elements. I practice deep breathing and get my energy in a state of pre-caffeinated balance before venturing out into the day's cycles and spirals.

Your routine doesn't have to be anything extravagant. If you don't already have a daily practice of intentional alignment, consider starting small and working from there. Maybe you will do a week of one-minute daily devotion and increase it to five minutes the next week and ten minutes the next. Do what works best for you, but make sure to be consistent. It's all about consistency! Play with pushing your limits of dedication little by little, ensuring that every prayer, every breath, and every motion is meaningful to you personally.

Daily devotionals should *not* be stressful or obligatory; they should be something you *want* to do and something that helps you shine as a better and more fulfilled person in daily life. If you feel that the dedications are becoming burdensome, take a break and return to them when you're feeling more confident in the work.

### The Value of Meditation

In addition to prayers and yoga, empaths greatly benefit from meditation. Meditation is something that I personally need to practice more often—as my brother Arun from India is often quick to point out! It's easy to get accustomed to a daily routine of alignment that involves physical movement and activity. Perhaps this is because most people perform daily dedications after waking up and getting showered, making it feel counterintuitive to meditate, as we want to avoid falling back to sleep!

Depending on the person, meditation in either the morning or the evening is more effective. It is worth experimenting with both times and deciding what works best for you. For those who work an early job, it may be better to meditate in the evening because the mind will not be so distracted with time limitations and daily obligations.

In a Buddhist meditation course I attended at the University of Montana, we were taught that meditation is not about emptying the mind but is designed to align the body, mind, and spirit as one fully functioning system of health. This alignment can promote all-inclusive health and happiness.

One of the first meditative techniques I was taught involves counting the breath. Once seated in a comfortable position with eyes closed, breathe normally and bring your focus to the in-breath. Notice where the oxygen enters your nose, and count your inhalations to thirty. Follow this by shifting your focus to where the breath exits your nose, and count your exhalations to thirty. Conclude by focusing on the brief moment of time in between each inhalation and exhalation, also to a count of thirty.

Others find it beneficial to meditate while chanting 108 mantras, perhaps using a mala or rosary. Even a simple *Om* or an uplifting English word such as *joy* or *strength* can go a long way in setting an encouraging mood for the day, spiritually and psychologically. Other meditators will intentionally focus on compassion, oneness, universal light, and love for their household, family, community, country, and the world. In my Buddhist meditation class, I was able to experience the benefit of a cloudlike mind: any time a thought, judgment, or worry would pop in my head, I would visualize it surrounded by a little fluffy cloud drifting off in the breeze. This practice allows the mind to dismiss stressful thoughts and return to a place of equanimity.

Some folks, especially in the Western world, find it easier to slip into a meditative state by following instructional visualizations or listening to either spoken words or meditative music. An incredible number of guided meditations and meditative music can be found on YouTube and other sources. If it helps your practice, consider pulling up some of these video and audio instructionals to find your own routine. With practice, you may find that you no longer need to rely on external tools.

---

*Daily devotionals should not be stressful or obligatory; they should be something you want to do and something that helps you shine as a better and more fulfilled person in daily life. If you feel that the dedications are becoming burdensome, take a break and return to them when you're feeling more confident in the work.*

---

### Shrines and Sacred Space

Many spiritual people naturally resonate with the concept of a shrine or sacred space. It's calming on many levels to have a special spot set aside for meditation, prayer, and spiritual focus. Shrines can take numerous forms and are limited only by one's imagination.

Various religions make use of shrines that are constructed in very particular arrangements consistent with ancient practices. Shrines and altars seen in churches and temples around the world usually follow these precise patterns, while those set up in one's home or office can be a bit more freeform.

If you prefer to work with particular deities, saints, spirits, or ancestors, it's a good idea to set up a shrine (or multiple shrines) with those focused intentions. Many spiritual people also like to construct shrines that display special items found in nature alongside other spiritual items such as candles, incense, bells, feathers, statues, crystals, herbs, shells, mementos, and family photographs. There is no wrong way to set up a shrine or altar; the most important thing is that you maintain the space by keeping it free of clutter and dust and regularly change it so the energies don't become stagnant.

Empaths, psychics, and other sensitive individuals can find great benefit in spending time at their sacred shrine on a daily basis. This helps intentionally reconnect us to life's bigger picture, giving us the opportunity to get out of our head for a bit and link our psyche to forces greater than ourselves.

### Vision Boards and Affirmations

One popular method of setting an intention in a focused manner is to construct vision boards. These pieces of art can be as organized or random as you wish and can be focused on one goal or many. Vision boards are representations of these wishes in the form of words, drawings, photos, and other items that represent the intention. A vision board is usually constructed by starting with a base of poster board or an artist's canvas. By adding various components, words, and imagery to the pieces, we can focus on the ideals and help them become more prominent in the conscious mind. This is believed to aid in the manifestation of these goals in the real world.

Vision boards help us put thoughts into form. Empaths can create vision boards that evoke the emotional energy of the goal. When emotionalizing the goal with images of happy people, for example, our brain's mirror neurons are triggered toward a positive response. Our brains are programmed to seek happiness and comfort and to avoid potentially painful experiences. By displaying uplifting emotions alongside other imagery related to the goal, vision boards help us take steps more joyously toward actualizing our ambitions.

Another way to reset your natural rhythm is to use positive affirmations, which are short phrases that affirm something positive, such as "I affirm that I am safe, I am loved, and I am valuable to this world." Louise Hay, founder of Hay House Publishing, was one of the foremost proponents of the power of affirmations, and many of her inspirational books and oracle cards strongly promote their healing power.

Experiment with creating your own positive affirmations, and make an effort to utilize them on a daily basis. When affirmations are coupled with work on vision boards, your goals become difficult to ignore and much easier to manifest!

### Everyday Empathic Techniques

Here are some ideas for readers who wish to incorporate a daily routine into their lives or to enhance a routine that is already under way. These practices are invaluable for empathic souls because they can clear accumulated energies and invite new vibrations into each daily cycle.

- **Light a candle:** Every spiritual system across the world values the fiery flame because it embodies nature's transformative element that turns raw food into nourishment, coldness into warmth, and darkness into light. Even a small candle flame is deeply symbolic of our human desire to commune with the divine, which is why numerous prayers, spells, and other intentional spiritual acts are enriched by the presence of a candle. When you light your candle, set an intention for the day. Dedicate the flame to a purpose. Make your affirmation known to the universe. Then go about your day. (If you are leaving the house for any reason, be sure to fully extinguish the candle first.)

- **Play some inspiring music:** It can be refreshing and empowering to play some tunes with which you feel a special spiritual identification, whether they are vocal or nonvocal. Branch out and discover similar works of sonic art that are related to the music you most enjoy. Indulging in music while you get ready for the day or while winding down can invoke a sacred and more aligned level of consciousness. Music can be empathically cathartic and therapeutic, to say the least!

- **Smudge with sage:** Smudging with sage is much more than a New Age practice of cleansing energy. Practitioners of various Native American religions often burn sage, sweetgrass, and other sacred herbs together in order to commune with the ancestors, spirits, and the Creator. The ancient Celts also utilized sage for spiritual and medicinal purposes. Wherever sage grows, it has been used, and understandably so; most varieties of sage smell sweet and serene when dried and burned. If it is beneficial to your daily practice, smudge yourself and your environment before or after the daily grind. You may also wish to do the same with some all-natural incense that puts you in a spiritual frame of mind. When smudging with any type of sacred herb, the billowing smoke can be waved around people, pets, items, or the house in order to help clear negative vibes or energy that is "stuck." The smoke can also be burned as an offering while you pray to spirits, guides, ancestors, gods, or other nonphysical entities.

- **Purify with salt water:** In order to cleanse your energy and remove any accumulated emotional buildup, create a saltwater blend at any ratio and sprinkle yourself with its grounding essence. Warm water helps the salt to dissolve faster, and while Himalayan pink salt is ideal for this purpose, any type of salt will do—even baking soda in a pinch! You may consider dumping warm salt water all over your body during or after a bath or shower. You may also incorporate an energy cleansing of your house, room, or property by simply mixing salt with water and sprinkling it throughout.

- **Enchant your breakfast:** It's common in spiritual cultures and communities to say a prayer or express gratitude to the universe before consuming a meal and, in many cases, before having any sort of drink or beverage—even water. By consciously giving thanks for the amazing food and drink that we have the luxury of consuming, we can remind ourselves of how beautiful it is to share life on this precious earth. You may also consider visualizing your food and drink bathed in white light or in a color that feels nourishing for your mind, body, and spirit. As you give thanks and lend enchanting energies to your food, remember that you—and indeed everyone on this planet—deserve health, sustenance, and wellness.

# The Healing Power of Nature

The world's greatest spiritual traditions are built upon a foundation that is interconnected with nature's mighty cycles. We can observe this spiritual reverence of nature when we look at the various holidays and festivals in longstanding religions. These special occurrences take place on an annual cycle that ensures a specific seasonal alignment; for example, Easter is always in the spring, intentionally placed right next to the vernal equinox.

The holidays of major religions almost always spring from earlier Pagan festivals. Pagan spirituality has always emphasized an immediate connection to the cycles of nature, so when newer religions take over, they naturally superimpose their religious festivals onto preexisting spiritual structures. This keeps things seasonal.

Regardless of religion, the natural world holds great sway over our emotions and deserves reverence! When we empaths immerse ourselves in nature and all she has to offer, we can discover a great sense of peace and healing. We can, in turn, offer a piece of our own energy to Mother Nature by practicing recycling and conscious eating and living as sustainably as possible.

## *Natural Cleansing*

A great way to cleanse our empathic senses is to journey into nature. The natural world is, of course, deeply studied and explored in scientific fields. Everything in nature has a biological purpose and function, even if we have yet to understand some of the intricacies. The plants, soil, water, and animals of any given area are interconnected and interdependently linked.

Some of us don't have to travel far to be in nature, but for empaths who live in big cities, nature can be a place of comfort and refuge. So often we are inundated with people, with fast-paced energy, with constant obligations, and with schedules, schedules, schedules! Sometimes we literally need to schedule time aside to reset ourselves in nature. A hike in the mountains can do wonders for the spirit!

Speaking of big-city energy, I remember my most recent trips to the Los Angeles area. I was raised in and currently live in a smaller city of about 75,000 people, so trips to bigger cities are always a bit overwhelming—but a fun change of pace! My trips to Southern California usually tend to be book-signing tours or something media-related, as well as opportunities to see old and dear friends. I stayed with a good friend in West Hollywood on my most recent journey, and with someone else in Inglewood on the trip before that, and with another good friend in Granada Hills on a trip a few years prior. Although these areas are a ways apart, they are interconnected in the grand scheme of LA. Funny enough, the same thing happened to me in each of these locations: as I lay down to sleep, I became bombarded with awkward visions of shapeshifting faces. The faces that appeared in my mind's eye were impeccably clear down to the detail. Each face appeared for a few seconds and then shifted into another face entirely—faces I'd never seen—as if each one was a ghost passing through. None of them seemed to notice me. This has never happened to me in any other environment, so I'm convinced it's the energy of the area. Big cities with big histories are believed to accumulate spiritual energies, and spirits themselves, which sometimes have trouble moving on to the next world.

Experiences such as these remind me why natural environments are so special for empaths, psychics, and energetically sensitive individuals. Away from the to-and-fro of city life, nature unfolds at its own pace in a seamless and wondrous spiral dance. When empaths immerse themselves in nature for any period of time, our energies make a palpable shift to a slower and more blissful rhythm. Nature affects us mentally, emotionally, and physically all at once, thereby also affecting us spiritually.

Both fresh air and flowing water release a great number of negatively charged ions. Negative ions, which are bulked-up oxygen molecules or atoms, are not negative in a bad sense—quite the opposite! These naturally occurring particles affect our mind and emotions by preventing pollutants from staying airborne, allowing our body to more acutely absorb and process *pure* energy. Negative ions beneficially influence our nervous system, circulatory system, and digestive system all at once, and provide an all-natural antidepressant.

*Some of us don't have to travel far to be in nature, but for empaths who live in big cities, nature can be a place of comfort and refuge. So often we are inundated with people, with fast-paced energy, with constant obligations, and with schedules, schedules, schedules! Sometimes we literally need to schedule time aside to reset ourselves in nature. A hike in the mountains can do wonders for the spirit!*

### Everyday Empathic Techniques

Let's examine a few different environments and consider ways in which each climate can affect the empath. Consider experimenting with different environments in order to discover in which conditions you feel the most alignment or healing.

- **Forests:** Depending on which time of year and which area we visit, mountainous and forested environments can be pleasurable turfs or treacherous terrains. In warmer circumstances, we can especially feel the aliveness of nature's presence. When trees and naturally occurring structures surround us, we can't help but feel humbled by it all. The profundity of nature can feel overwhelming and disorienting at times, so it's a good idea to pace ourselves and to know where we are at all times (in proximity to the car or to the road, for example). Certainly part of this magic is linked to the fact that the trees and plants around us are producing fresh oxygen for us to absorb. Forests can do wonders for resetting ourselves empathically, especially if we journey to a lake, river, waterfall, hot spring, or other watery environment.

- **Beaches:** Beaches produce a plentiful number of negative ions, which is why we feel so relaxed and content after a trip to the beach—even if we don't swim! An experience in this environment gives empaths an opportunity to reflect on how the element of water aligns with our emotions and empathic gifts. The sand on the beach reminds us that our planet is but one speck of the infinite universe. Also, who doesn't like to swim? By immersing ourselves in the sacred water, we can spiritually cleanse our emotions and reconnect to our primordial evolutionary roots; conscious life emerged from the ocean, after all!

• **Deserts:** Arid climates may sometimes appear barren and sterile, but in reality there is a subtly vibrant ecosystem that many plants and animals call home. A visit to such a warm environment can allow us to soak up the vitamin D in solar rays, which can help contribute to a more optimistic outlook. Many desert or desertlike climates can be hot in the daytime and bitter cold at night. These climates are ideal for reflecting on the dual nature of reality: light and dark, yin and yang, hot and cold. By far, the most magical time to visit a desert-like environment is at sunrise or sunset!

• **Tropics:** There is something profoundly magical about tropical environments. Indeed, there is more *prana* (life-force energy) surrounding us than we know what to do with! Moist and nourishing, tropical flora release fresh oxygen and surround our bodies with negative ions. Lush fruits and flowers emerge year round, showing us how generous Mother Nature can be. These environments hold a special place for emotionally sensitive folks because their lushness and humidity give rise to a feeling of safety and sustenance on numerous levels.

• **Cold climates:** Much like desert climates, a cold and snowy landscape can feel almost lifeless. With few plants and animals visible, snowy and icy environments can make a person feel a bit out of place. Still, the calmness of these environments is incomparable. A fresh blanket of snow can evoke a hypnotically lulling feeling of stillness. It's good for empaths to reflect on the metaphysical nature of frozen water. As water is linked with emotions, it makes sense to regard frozen water as an energy of emotional suspension; something changing at a slower pace. These environments can help us contemplate deeper emotions that we may be allowing to stagnate within us, while the solemnity of the environment can assist with introspection.

## *Minerals and Gemstones for Empaths*

Spiritual seekers of all varieties are aware that nature's gifts hold potent energies that we can tap into. For example, nature produces an abundance of herbs that can medically target anything under the sun. Naturopaths and herbal healers across the world help preserve the wisdom of medicinal herbs, plants, and oils. Ancient cultures and those who preserve ancient teachings also perpetuate old beliefs about the magical, metaphysical, and superstitious properties of plants—carry a four-leaf clover in your wallet to attract money, for example.

Stones are similar metaphysically, with various cultures and energy workers ascribing different energetic properties to certain minerals. Everything in nature carries a certain vibration, a unique essence. When we examine different spiritual belief systems, we see that a number of minerals and gemstones carry energetic qualities that can be empathically beneficial. Most strong empaths are metaphysically inclined to one degree or another, so experimenting with nature's gifts can be a fun and rewarding way to help us in our journey toward emotional equilibrium.

## *Everyday Empathic Techniques*

Here is a list of some of the most prominent gemstones successfully utilized by empaths for purposes related to our enhanced emotional capabilities. You may consider playing around with different combinations of stones to see which work best for you. I prefer to work with one stone at a time, while others enjoy the energy of combining vibrations.

Minerals and gemstones can be worked with by carrying them on your person, by placing them around the home, or by meditating with them in hand. Please be sure that the stones you acquire are *ethically produced* through noninvasive mining practices and nonexploitive working conditions. This may take a bit of research and a bit of talking to store owners, but it is absolutely worth it ethically and empathically.

- **Amethyst:** No doubt one of the most popular gemstones on the market, amethyst has a calming energy that can soothe even the most emotionally exhausted individual. Amethyst carries loving and peaceful vibrations that can help settle— and prevent—emotional distress.

- **Carnelian:** Renowned as a stone that helps inspire confidence, carnelian can be carried, worn, or placed on the body to help dispel anxieties and insecurities—two things that are all too familiar to highly empathic souls! Carnelian is also believed to promote peace, amicability, and emotional healing.

- **Chrysoprase:** This green form of chalcedony is believed to shield its wearers from all manner of external negativity. Chrysoprase additionally helps the wearer remain a bit more balanced in chaotic conditions while helping replace stressful energies with optimism.

- **Citrine:** Citrine is said to be a highly projective, protective, and radiant stone. Citrine's bright yellow color gives it metaphysical alignments to the sun, whose boisterous and life-giving energy is beneficial for empaths of all varieties.

This stone is also said to be resistant to absorbing energies, helping introverted empaths invoke a bit of extroverted courageousness.

- **Hematite:** Believed to be one of the best stones for grounding energy, hematite has a dense, dark, and sleek appearance that is also strikingly beautiful. Some empaths carry or wear hematite on a daily basis in order to stay anchored in the body rather than getting lost in emotional tangents of thought. It is common for people to utilize a piece of hematite for a period of time and then, after they feel it has absorbed too much external energy, bury the stone or toss it in a body of water. Alternatively, it can be cleansed with sage, salt water, sunlight, or moonlight.

- **Moonstone:** Few stones compare in beauty to true moonstone. In many cultures, the moon represents the soft, internal landscape of emotion and mystery. Empaths can utilize moonstone to help stay connected to their emotions in a healthy and spiritual manner.

- **Obsidian:** This beautiful stone is said to be an excellent protector against external negativity and is a great stone to wear when visualizing empathically protective shields. Like hematite and other black stones, obsidian is best utilized for a period of time until it feels as though it has absorbed an excess of external energy.

- **Petrified wood:** Technically a fossil, petrified wood is the result of water-based minerals permeating a submerged piece of wood over millions of years. Few things compare to the vibration of petrified wood, which connects us to the earth's primordial waters with incredible profundity. We can utilize petrified wood to keep us emotionally grounded and help us persevere through life's ebbs and flows.

• **Salt:** Salt of all types is said to help cleanse stagnant energies and create a rampart of protection. Salt can be used in the bath or shower and even carried in a spritz to instantly cleanse energy, should the need arise. Rock salt, sea salt, Himalayan pink salt, and other forms of salt and sodium each have their own vibrational essence and unique properties.

• **Seashells:** Seashells provide an energetic link to the mighty ocean and life's greater purpose. Seeing as empaths are connected to the element of water, seashells can help us stay emotionally connected. Because shells themselves are exoskeletons, their naturally protective properties can help us in our own construction of energetic shields.

• **Tourmaline (black):** Nothing can compare to the protective energy of black tourmaline, easily the most renowned stone for empaths! Frequently worn or carried by empaths and psychics in social situations, black tourmaline is specifically believed to protect its wearer from external emotional influences. By keeping outside emotions at bay, the wearer can maintain emotional equilibrium in public situations. Black tourmaline is best utilized only in public and only as necessary because of how strong a barrier it can create between the wearer and others.

### *Exercise:* An Empath's Charm Bag

Spiritual traditions across time and space have long utilized charm bags in some way, shape, or form. Empaths of all types can make use of charm bags designed for emotional protection.

This short exercise gives suggestions for components you can include in your own bag, but please feel free to modify the ingredients based on your own preferences and intuition. The energies of the herbs, stones, and items suggested here have been time-tested for emotional assistance in a variety of cultures.

Be sure to record the ingredients of your charm bag in your journal so you can look back and examine the contents. Make note of the bag's effects when you carry it in different social settings, including when you're on the phone and online, and decide which scenarios are the most ideal to utilize its magic. You may also wish to use the bag in meditation, especially when visualizing shields of emotional protection and when performing metaphysical work for emotional safety.

1. Use your intuition and best judgment to find an ideal bag. Small drawstring bags made of natural material are ideal for charm bags, especially if they are handmade. You may also consider trying your hand at stitching or sewing a small bag with one end open that you can bind or stitch together upon completion.

2. Begin your charm bag by adding a spoonful of sea salt. Sea salt comes from the ocean, of course, so it carries the significance of emotional connection due to its watery nature. For similar reasons, add a small seashell of some type. Cowrie shells are some of the most prevalent shells utilized metaphysically, but use your intuition to decide what "wants" to go in there to assist with your charm bag of emotional protection.

3. Focus on the watery presence of the sea salt and the seashell. Hold the bag to your heart and envision it surrounded in soft blues, whites, and greens. Think about how the

world's oceans connect to your own emotional tides, and mentally give thanks to the element of water.

4. If available, add a bit of the dried herb yarrow to the bag. Yarrow is said to be especially beneficial for empaths because its energy helps define boundaries, especially emotional ones. If you have access to the herbs rue or cinquefoil, these also have a long history in folk magic as being emotionally protective. Add pinches of a few other herbs you intuitively feel called toward, perhaps lavender, thyme, or sage.

5. Hold the bag to your brow, envisioning it surrounded with the colors indigo and white. Affirm that the bag is designed to aid in emotional protection, giving you the power to discern emotionally healthy situations from those that are not beneficial. Envision the herbs coming alive with these colors and aiding in your intention. Give thanks.

6. Add a black stone or stones to the bag that are said to be beneficial for empaths, such as hematite, black onyx, or black tourmaline. As a general rule, darker stones are best for helping secure energetic boundaries.

7. Press the charm bag to the base of your spine, envisioning the bag surrounded with earthy browns and greens. See these colors as protective vibrations that keep you grounded and connected to Mother Earth. Visualize the stone or stones in the bag coming alive with sacred properties of emotional protection while you give thanks to the mighty earth beneath your feet.

8. Conclude by adding any additional items to the bag that you feel called toward. This might include items found in nature,

good luck charms you've accumulated, medallions, feathers, and even written affirmations or prayers for protection.

9. Allow the bag to sit on a windowsill or in a safe place outside where it can absorb sunlight and moonlight, which will help its energy attune to the rhythm of nature. When you feel the time is right, start utilizing the bag in different situations and see how it affects your energy as an empath.

chapter eight

# Live to Serve

Within India's ancient spiritual traditions, such as Hinduism, Sikhism, Jainism and Buddhism, we find a special emphasis on the concept of *seva*. This Sanskrit word refers to selfless service without expectation of return or reward. The act of seva is an empath's most powerful offering to the world.

The path of yoga consists of numerous lifestyle disciplines, only one of which is the physical body postures within hatha yoga. According to Vedic traditions, performing seva in any form is an act of karma yoga. This is to say that selfless service to others helps resolve one's accumulated negative karmic imprints from this lifetime and prior ones. Karma yoga is energetic purification. Nonprofit volunteer work, for example, is an act of karma yoga.

When we approach the concept of seva, it's okay to have the awareness that the service is karmically beneficial for ourselves, although the focus should be directed primarily toward those who are being helped. Most importantly, we must actually *want* to help others in need. Whereas this selflessness may be a struggle for many people, this desire comes pretty easily to those who are highly empathetic. We can ride the wave of seva by taking note of the feeling of *fulfillment* that is borne of helping others, whether human, animal, environmental, or otherwise.

For those who practice healing professions of any variety, there is most definitely an additional need to make an income. There is no shame in this reciprocity if the rates and expectations are ethical. While this type of exchange may not be seva in the truest sense, if the practitioner's primary focus is successful healing rather than focusing on what they receive in return, the karmic energy at hand is in positive alignment. Still, even people who work in healing fields would be advised to practice deeper seva by sometimes offering their skills pro bono to individuals in need.

However we choose to serve the world, focusing our attention on "the other" yields the greatest results. We empaths are here to help the world and its inhabitants however we are able.

-----

*According to Vedic traditions, performing seva in any form is an act of karma yoga. This is to say that selfless service to others helps resolve one's accumulated negative karmic imprints from this lifetime and prior ones. Karma yoga is energetic purification.*

## Sharing Our Gifts

At times it may feel like our empathic abilities are more challenging than they are special, but truth be told, empaths are natural healers. I would argue that empathy's purpose in the world is to inspire unity, growth, and healing, so it's only reasonable to assume that we empaths are meant to do this to the best of our ability.

When we are emotionally balanced, we feel on top of the world and can navigate anything that life throws our way. When we choose to work on ourselves, we can more accurately serve others in various ways. This service can be psychological, emotional, spiritual, or (most likely) a combination of these elements. Empathic healing can take the form of something as formal as medical care to something as informal as chatting with a friend over coffee. Empaths are natural healers of different expressions. Healing is part of what we are here to do. This is our place in the world. Sharing love and compassion is not only one of our abilities but also our responsibility.

### Emotional Compartmentalization

Not too long ago I found myself in a hospital emergency room with someone I care about greatly. They had suffered a kitchen accident and I was there to lend assistance to the best of my ability. The injury, while being treated, was causing severe pain. Empathically, it was difficult to keep my own tears at bay while offering support. During this process, I also witnessed medical professionals engaging in "emotional compartmentalization" tactics. In other words, they would offer empathetic and soothing words briefly and then swiftly snap back into action as medics. They simply disallowed emotions to override the cognitive focus required for medical attentiveness. Without question, this is a method that a wide variety of medics use across the world.

The witnessing of this approach also brought to mind other instances in the past when I may have witnessed this behavior and chalked it up to thinking the medics were cold or emotionally fragmented. Now, as a more developed empath, I see that some amount of emotional separation is required for objective and accurate triage, diagnosis, and treatment. There are times when we empaths must remember the benefit of this method when the going gets tough. We do not want to be like this *all* the time, but on occasion it can be greatly beneficial.

During this recent medical excursion, I was reminded of instances in the past when I was present during similar incidents. In the past, I had the tendency to empathically absorb the painful, confused, and fearful energy exuded by individuals in emergency situations. With my empathic skills running amok, uncontrolled, I allowed these difficult emotions into my own sphere and became overwhelmed, discombobulated, stressed, and panicked. This, of course, was not beneficial for myself or the other parties at the time. In fact, it was a great challenge to realize how to help the individuals in need.

During this more recent incident, I decided to purposefully change my approach when the kitchen injury first occurred. First, I recognized that there was a problem that required a solution. Next, I quickly made an agreement with my higher self *not* to get emotionally attached to the other party's emotional pain (which was a result from the physical pain experienced). I realized that this empathically absorptive approach would not be helpful for them or anyone involved. I chose to keep my problem-solving energy restricted to the mental sphere instead of becoming whisked away by my own emotional disarray. After making observational assessments and the appropriate phone calls, I was able to accurately assist with the situation in that moment. It was far more helpful to formulate a plan of action and provide assistance with *sympathy* by saying things like "be strong, deep breaths, hang in there," until the problem was fully addressed.

This allowed me to emotionally process the experience *later,* after the necessary treatment was provided.

Emotional compartmentalization, when needed, is much easier said than done for us empaths, but it can be the most beneficial course of action when helping those who are experiencing emergency situations. Just remember that the pendulum doesn't have to swing fully to one side or the other; there is no need for us to be fully hot or fully cold at any given time. When we are intellectually assisting others through problem solving, we can still offer emotional support with brief words of consolation and encouragement. We can still have an emotional presence without diving headfirst into the ultimately *un*helpful depths of full-on empathy in an urgent situation. Just the same, we do not have to shut off our rational thinking when emotionally processing traumatic experiences with others, whether the trauma was our own or someone else's. Although we have the ability to fluctuate between the mental and emotional spheres, we don't have to entirely engulf ourselves in one or the other; we have a responsibility to maintain our composure to the best of our ability when we are helping others in need.

### What Is a Healer?

Empathic healing work takes so many forms, and every healer has one or more specialties that simply take a bit of research (and experience) to discover. Because so many healing disciplines are available, a journey into the healing arts can be a monumentally large task. So take it one step at a time and enjoy the process!

Think about what the word *healer* means to you (ideally with your journal in hand!). From your point of view, what *are* professional healers and how do they practice? How can this term be applied to individuals who may not carry the title "healer" themselves, such as educators, clergy members, or those who work in social services? How can this term be expanded even further to encompass individuals who may not necessarily practice healing within their chosen profession? And, most importantly, how can *you* incorporate deeper healing for others into your own lifestyle—including your occupation, whatever it may be—and what sorts of life changes can you make in order to deepen and expand this healing even further?

---

*Empathic healing can take the form of something as formal as medical care to something as informal as chatting with a friend over coffee. Empaths are natural healers of different expressions. Healing is part of what we are here to do. This is our place in the world. Sharing love and compassion is not only one of our abilities but also our responsibility.*

## Methods of Service

Everything in life is a give-and-take. The act of healing service is not restricted to a realm of professional formality. Instead, healing work takes place constantly, every day! Even the smallest of interactions can provide healing for others, even if we don't realize it at the time.

I can't count the number of times that a tarot client has returned to me years after a reading simply to tell me how much my empathetic advice was helpful in their life. What an honor! This sort of confirmation reminds me that even everyday conversations can have a lasting impact on another person's psyche and emotions. This also reminds me to keep my shadow side in check constantly, because damaging interactions can have an equally intense impact on another person's wellbeing. These positive and negatives also have an echo effect in that the imprints we leave on another person can influence the energies that they project onto others throughout daily life. That's a lot of responsibility!

The energy of empathic healing and social service is unrestricted, being deeply interwoven with our everyday experience. When we empaths continually remind ourselves that we are in fact natural healers, our everyday interactions can more easily be fueled with a dedication toward helping elevate others out of darkness.

### *Serving Friends, Family, and Colleagues*

When it comes to those closest to us, we empaths can let down our guard quite a bit more than we might do with strangers or acquaintances. With close family members, friends, and romantic partners, we naturally have a certain emotional proximity that allows us to open up with those whose trust has been established. Emotional safety has to be proven and earned, so it's greatly fulfilling to know that we have individuals in our lives whom we care about and who genuinely care for us in return.

Ironically, we empaths can sometimes be overly critical of or harsh toward those we feel closest to. This is perhaps because the relationship has become familiar or routine. We may worry less about the consequences of our behavior when it comes to interacting with those we feel closest to—they'll always be there, right? It's important to remember that individuals with whom we have built an emotional rapport *deserve* that connectedness if they consistently offer it in return. Close friends and family members are the individuals with whom we should endeavor to uphold the greatest amount of empathy, especially during times of conflict.

It is vital to maintain empathy throughout the home in every way possible. Parents must educate their children and families about the importance of empathy. When interacting with children in particular, it's a good idea to encourage a lot of "I feel" statements. This inspires kids to communicate emotionally rather than simply be reactive. "I feel" statements require a brief moment of self-examination, naturally producing a bit more emotional awareness in the individual. When emotional communication becomes habitual, even the most difficult interactions can become heartfelt, humble, and bonding.

Our interactions with colleagues, associates, and coworkers are also of great importance. While we may converse with them in a different manner than with our friends and family, it's important to stay true to our feelings in all types of social situations. If you believe that everything happens for a reason, then there is a purpose behind your interactions with colleagues—and also with total strangers!

Some of these interactions can really challenge us empathetically. Because we don't necessarily spend time outside of work with coworkers, the relationships will be a bit different and are likely to embody a mixture of job-based communication coupled with some degree of personal disclosure. In highly social jobs, we all have to work with individuals from many different backgrounds and who are prone to a wide variety of emotional responses or the lack thereof. Promoting compassionate understanding is beneficial for the workplace as a whole; you *do* have an effect on your occupational environment, even if it doesn't always seem that way.

When interacting with colleagues, acquaintances, strangers, and others with whom you haven't developed a highly emotional bond, it's wise not to reveal too much about your personal life or to communicate potentially controversial opinions. It can take a while to develop good working relationships, so it's healthy to exercise a bit of caution. Communicative boundaries with each person are best gauged by observing their *own* level of emotional comfort, which can help you determine ways in which you can comfortably interact without pushing too many boundaries. After all, it's an empath's duty to help keep the peace!

### Volunteerism and Community Service

The practice of helping others in need can be the most profound, emotionally uplifting experience in the world. Selfless service truly is a win-win situation!

We can so easily get lost in our head, circling around emotional labyrinths and mental whirlpools. We know this. When we give our time and energy to those who need it most, we can actually get out of our head for a while and feel good about it. There's a unique and special sensation that results when we feel accomplished and feel as though we are doing *good work*. This is the feeling we should all be going for; it is the feeling of being aligned with our higher purpose.

A giving personality is something we can choose to demonstrate 24/7. Naturally, we mustn't allow ourselves to get taken advantage of and must maintain a levelheaded sense of boundaries. We cannot allow other people's energies to overtake us, and we cannot allow ourselves to give our energy where it's rejected.

When we make up our mind to give energy to those who dearly need it, we discover that a simple smile or compliment can totally change a person's day for the better. Once we as empaths realize just how capable we are of generating emotional healing, a generous nature becomes something we sincerely strive to embody.

### Everyday Empathic Techniques

Volunteer work and giving back can take numerous forms, including the following broad categories. It is advisable to experiment with a variety of volunteer avenues to see where you fit in. Everyone has different callings!

- **Nature work:** There are many ways to lend help to the environment in your local community. If you live in a college town, you may wish to contact the environmental sciences department of your local university to inquire about nature-based volunteer work. This can include anything from picking up litter to planting trees. You may also consider volunteering at a local food co-op, recycling center, or community-based agricultural collective.

- **Animal work:** Without a voice to speak up for themselves, animals are some of society's most vulnerable members. It's our responsibility to help them however we can. When choosing to embark on work with animals, think about your options. Perhaps you feel drawn toward working with shelters, fighting for farm-based welfare, or becoming an advocate for spaying and neutering.

- **Humanitarian work:** There are individuals in need throughout literally every part of the world—every country, every region, and every city. Research local humanitarian organizations and think about nonprofit charities that help individuals in need.

Suggestions for volunteering your time, energy, and empathy include homeless shelters, soup kitchens, churches, nursing homes, organizations for those with disabilities, battered women's shelters, volunteer firefighting and EMT organizations, displaced children's homes, human rights networks, political activist groups, anti-circumcision organizations, and so many other possibilities.

### Exercise: *Think Global, Act Local*

Here at the nonprofit multicultural temple and farm that I co-operate in beautiful Missoula, Montana, we are big advocates of the phrase "Think global, act local." This philosophy becomes more widespread every day as advocates for human rights, animal rights, and environmental rights seek to educate the masses on ways they can help the world rather than fall victim to its harshness.

Sometimes it feels like there's nothing we can do to help others in need around the world, but in truth there is always *something*—some letter to write, some politician to call, some petition to sign, some activist group to join, some charity to donate to, something to protest, some candle to light, some prayer to be uttered … There's always a way to help, even if it feels small.

This exercise encourages readers to think outside the box. We are exposed to so much information in this day and age, and all this input can be incredibly overwhelming. This is especially true when we observe the news. Emotions are conveyed in every news story, regardless of the source. Metaphysical folks might say that we actually tap into a greater emotional well of other readers' or viewers' energies when we read or view evocative news stories. A great way for empaths to process some of this emotional information is to get active and do something about it.

You, dear reader, may feel passionate about issues that are different from those that I myself feel passionate about. That's wonderful! I strongly believe that everyone is called to different causes for a reason. We all have emotional specialties in different arenas. With all of our work being done together through different avenues, we can collectively help relieve suffering across the world.

Even if corrupt individuals in influential political or corporate positions seem to be the ones in control, remember that this idea is part of our social conditioning. Why would they want us to feel otherwise? Why would they want us to become aware of our power and of the progressive influence we can inspire from the ground up? Keep in mind that every positive action has a ripple effect; we are subtly influencing those "in power" with every contagious act of goodness we perform.

When we are fighting for righteous global causes, it's great to do work that helps those souls in need. However, even if we've signed the petitions, made the phone calls, and said the prayers, we may be left with an aching feeling of "What else can I do?" That's where this exercise comes into play.

When we think globally, we instantly tap into the energy of another location. We can help to some extent from our position in the world, but sometimes we feel called toward a bit more action. Therefore, we must bring about the next step: acting locally.

1. Spend some time with your journal this week. Find out what's going on globally by watching the news, reading the news, and talking with others about the news. Brace yourself when learning about the horrors of the world; it's easy

for empaths to neglect global updates because of how altogether *sad* they can be. However, even if it's difficult to emotionally separate ourselves from them, we must be informed about world events if we want to exercise a positive influence.

2. Take note of different worldwide occurrences discussed in the news. Jot down the date and a brief summary of each emotionally evocative news story. How does each report make you feel, and what is your greatest aspiration for the subjects of the story? How would you help them if you were there in that situation?

3. When you feel especially overcome with emotion about certain stories reported in the news, take a little time to sit in a darkened room and meditate. Visualize the individuals, animals, and/or environments involved surrounded by a supportive white healing light. Surround them with this protection and speak positive affirmations to their spirits; maybe some part of them can feel you. Light a candle and focus your positive intentions through the flame. If you are familiar with Reiki or other forms of energy work, send those good vibrations through the flame and through the astral web that connects us all. Breathe, pray, and have hope.

4. As previously discussed, take a bit of real-world action if you are able to in any way, whether it's signing a petition, writing to a member of Congress, and even spreading the news story across social media platforms. This will help get the ball rolling in the right direction. You may even find

suggestions for assistance in a news story's comments section online or within the article itself.

5. In order to bring this global perspective to a place of grounding, act locally. Think about different organizations and causes that exist in your area, and do some good, solid research to see who's out there. Which of these organizations actively work in a field that targets similar issues to those featured in the news stories toward which you had an emotional response?

6. Next, touch base. Contact organizations who work locally on global causes that you feel called to assist. For example, if you encounter an emotional news story about abandoned children, contact your local child welfare offices and related charities to see how you can lend volunteer assistance or even pursue a career in the field. Continue this work in other ways with different local organizations that pursue action related to your global callings.

7. When you call any given organization or stop by their offices, be honest; tell them that you feel motivated to help because you believe in the work they're doing. Schedule time with these local groups and ensure that you follow through. Even if it's a only couple hours a month, *everything* helps. When we all work locally, the empathic ripple truly becomes global.

# Conclusion

As we have explored in these pages, the everyday empath's key to living a balanced life begins with the self and ends with our influence in the world at large.

Even if we have empathically absorbed emotions from other people, the fact remains that our emotions are our own. It does no good to blame other people for our emotional wellbeing, because at the end of the day it's our decision how to process emotional information and move on with our lives. By accepting responsibility for our feelings and actions, we become more humbly self-aware and more receptive to emotional healing.

Everyone is unique and everyone is a developing empath. It's easy to compare ourselves to other people, wishing that we were better or more like someone else. These feelings are only human! For those of us with high levels of emotional sensitivity, the game of comparison can keep us from reaching our *own* true potential. While there is *always* room for self-improvement, the most significant thing we empaths can do is to have empathy for ourselves.

I've realized throughout the years that it's easy to advise other people, but it's another thing entirely to take that same advice on board personally. This is greatly due to the fact that not only are we our own worst critics, but we also tend to look past other people's faults and shortcomings more easily. It's far too easy for empaths to latch onto self-defeating beliefs. The remedy for this is forgiveness. We are not defined by our past, and there is no sense in holding on to things that we have already experienced and have learned from. We can choose to cultivate empathy for ourselves just as much as for others, even if it is much easier said than done.

During the inevitable times when you are feeling negative or hopeless, consider how you would advise another person in this situation. It's never easy to take a step back from our own mind and emotions, but the exercises presented in this book should make this process a bit easier. It takes time, but we are most certainly capable of shifting our subjective views to ones that are more beneficially objective.

Creating deeper empathy for ourselves can be achieved by imagining someone else in our scenario. Ask yourself, "If someone I love were in my shoes right now, how would I advise them?" This act of stepping back is a tried-and-true springboard for self-healing.

As you go about your life, it is my hope that you will keep in mind many of the perspectives and ideas offered in this book. It's one thing to read a few words in theory and another to activate those things in practice. It is likely that you will begin noticing the flow of empathic exchange throughout daily life, and you may even remember some of the points brought up in this book.

We greatly empower ourselves as empaths when we remember that we have a powerful influence on the world in everyday life. We are not mere emotional sponges; we are emotional alchemists!

Life isn't always easy, but let's remember what a great blessing it is to be experiencing consciousness, especially at this time in global history! We are literally forging an emotional trail that will continue to influence generations to come. Empathy is on the rise, and each of us can encourage its blossoming in the world on a daily basis. Although it sometimes feels as though our influence is small, the waters of empathy are deeply powerful. Empathy permeates time and space, actively working as a force of goodness that can overcome the evils of the world. World peace is directly linked to the encouragement of empathy. Our everyday thoughts, speech, and actions create an energetic ripple in the world's infinite pool of empathic unity, and it all starts with each of us.

### *Exercise:* Action for Animals

I feel that an excellent way to wrap up the prior exercises in this book is to step outside our inner landscape for a bit by bringing our focus to the sacred realm of animals. Animals of all types typically have a special place in the heart of the empath.

As I write this section, I find my eyes getting teary just thinking about how beautiful, pure, and compassionate animals can be. From the little mouse to the mighty elephant, animals embody nature's purity. Animals are extensions of nature's consciousness. The same holds true for humans, but our ego and enhanced self-awareness set our own embodiment of consciousness apart from other animals. Humans can be much more calculating and intelligent than other animals, for better or worse.

Sure, animals can be destructive, vicious, and predatory, but this is part of their nature. These are not traits that are wicked or abnormal. Like us, animals are products not only of nature but also of nurture and upbringing. If a cruel and wounded person has projected their own wounds onto their dog in the form of abuse, you're damn right that dog's going to have a fearful or aggressive personality due to personal experience.

True empaths could never imagine causing pain to an animal, a child, or any other innocent being. For many of us, such things are deeply unnerving, even incomprehensible. No wonder we are so affected by global news and stories of injustice. In our hearts, we *know* what is right and what is wrong.

If you do find yourself focusing on sad aspects of animal welfare, utilize the empathic transmutation techniques discussed earlier. Turn that influx of energy into an outpouring of love and fortitude for those souls in need. Don't just buckle down under the emotional pain—you are here to help bring the whole world to a higher frequency, like it or not!

This exercise can be emotionally challenging, as it involves utilizing empathy in a high-energy public setting. This time, however, very few humans are involved in the process. Instead, it is the animal realm with which we are forging bonds and sharing our empathic gifts.

For this exercise, you will want to set aside an afternoon to visit various animal shelters in your area. Do some research into which facilities are available for visitation locally, and take note of their hours. Shelters in my own area include the Humane Society, Animal Control, and a local nonprofit called Animeals. Each facility has its own operating hours, so it's essential to plan visitations in advance. Additionally, most animal shelters have *volunteer* hours, which could be ideal to incorporate into this exercise if you have the time and willingness to freely give.

Please also note that it is both customary and compassionate to give a financial donation of any amount when you visit an animal shelter. Please do what you can within your own means. Also, unless you are in the market to adopt a new pet, prepare yourself for each visitation by firmly agreeing *not* to adopt any of the beautiful animals you encounter. If it is time for you to adopt an animal companion, which I personally feel every empath needs, I wish you the best of luck finding the companion who is meant to be.

If you don't have an animal shelter in your area or don't feel entirely comfortable visiting one for the purpose of this exercise, consider some humanitarian organizations you can visit instead, such as a homeless shelter or soup kitchen. Although this exercise assumes that you will be visiting animal shelters, you are welcome to look around in your area for a more fitting alternative if you feel called to a different possibility.

1. Before you begin the exercise, perform protective visualizations that will help you throughout the experience. Because it can often be emotionally draining to see others in need—especially if you cannot help them directly—it's important to have your shields constructed. As we explored earlier in the book, everybody's method of energetic protection is different, so be sure to work with the visualizations, prayers, and meditations that you have found to be most helpful to you personally. When you feel prepared for the experience, proceed to the next step.

2. Once you visit the first shelter on your list (which may be the only shelter in your area or may be one of dozens, depending on where you live), check in with the staff and let them know that you simply wish to visit and pet the animals and are not looking to adopt (unless you are!). Most shelters will happily allow you to visit the animals in their enclosures, and many will even allow you to take cats to specialized play areas and walk dogs in a fenced outdoor space.

3. With hand sanitizer handy, which most animal shelters provide in abundance, slowly make your way from animal to animal. The majority of animals will be cats and dogs, some of which are lost runaways and others the result of overbreeding (*please* spay and neuter!), neglect, or abuse. These grim realities of these beautiful animals are often not socially propagated because they're unpleasant to think about. These particular animals have been blessed enough to land in the shelter you are visiting, which cannot be said for all.

4. While you slowly make your way among kitties, doggies, and other animals, you are likely to read their bios and learn their given names. As a strong empath with a big heart, you may cry at times during your visitation. Please be sure to bring tissues and try not to let this sadness overtake you. After all, this exercise is designed *for* empaths like you. The purpose of this is to find an emotional balance even when you feel relatively helpless in a situation. (Again, you may wish to consider volunteering regularly at animal shelters, because then you really would be making an immediate difference in the lives of many.)

5. As you visit a variety of animals, do your best not to absorb the traumatic emotional energy that you will sense some of them carrying. Utilize projective empathy to give care, love, and comfort while you pet them, talk to them, and communicate with them in your own way. Keep in mind that you are *brave* enough to confront potential emotional pain and transform it into something a bit ... lighter.

6. Although this is an empathic exercise, it is not primarily about you; it is about gifting light and love to these animals

despite the emotions that are welling up within you. As you visit each animal, you will notice their unique personalities and quirks. After your initial sadness has been consciously transformed, it will become more joyous and inspiring to visit every beautiful spirit.

7. Carry this energy onward to other shelters in your area in order to utilize your light-giving gifts as an empath with society's most vulnerable souls. As you offer love and light, it will also help the animals in their spirit's own quest to find the owner who is perfect for them and vice versa. You may also consider carrying on a similar practice by visiting elderly folks in nursing homes; this is a population that is in need of compassion while they take life's final steps. Many nursing homes also welcome pets and their owners to visit to provide therapeutic companionship and lighthearted enjoyment.

8. Finally, consider ways you can make positive changes in your own daily life that benefit animals you may not have personally met. For example, you may decide to only consume meat that is 100 percent humanely raised, sustainably produced, or ethically hunted. Maybe you'll even decide to go vegetarian or vegan if you're not already! You may decide to become somewhat of an activist or letter writer for judicial changes in animal welfare statutes. You may choose to host fundraising drives and events to assist organizations that help the animals, or you may choose to volunteer regularly at your local shelters. The possibilities are endless. By empathizing with the plight of truly innocent beings, our innermost empathic souls can thrive by way of selfless service and loving assistance. In this way, we are truly living our purpose.

# Further Reading

Aron, Elaine N. *The Highly Sensitive Person: How to Thrive When the World Overwhelms You.* Secaucus, NJ: Birch Lane Press, 1996.

Belanger, Michelle. *The Psychic Energy Codex: Awakening Your Subtle Senses.* San Francisco, CA: Red Wheel/Weiser, 2007.

Bennett, Michael J. *The Empathic Healer: An Endangered Species?* San Diego, CA: Academic Press, 2001.

Bennett-Goleman, Tara. *Emotional Alchemy: How the Mind Can Heal the Heart.* New York: Harmony Books, 2001.

Coyle, T. Thorn. *Kissing the Limitless: Deep Magic and the Great Work of Transforming Yourself and the World.* San Francisco, CA: Red Wheel/Weiser, 2009.

Dale, Cyndi. *The Spiritual Power of Empathy: Develop Your Intuitive Gifts for Compassionate Connection.* Woodbury, MN: Llewellyn, 2014.

De Waal, Frans. *The Age of Empathy: Nature's Lessons for a Kinder Society.* New York: Harmony Books, 2009.

Digitalis, Raven. *Esoteric Empathy: A Magickal & Metaphysical Guide to Emotional Sensitivity.* Woodbury, MN: Llewellyn, 2017.

Ekman, Paul. *Emotions Revealed: Recognizing Faces and Feelings to Improve Communication and Emotional Life.* New York: Holt, 2003.

Fitzhugh, Elisabeth Y. *Dancers Between Realms: Empath Energy, Beyond Empathy.* Waynesboro, VA: Synchronicity Press, 2006.

Fortune, Dion. *Psychic Self-Defense: The Classic Instruction Manual for Protecting Yourself Against Paranormal Attack.* San Francisco, CA: Red Wheel/Weiser, 2011.

Goldie, Peter, ed. *The Oxford Handbook of Philosophy of Emotion.* New York: Oxford University Press, 2010.

Goleman, Daniel. *Emotional Intelligence: Why It Can Matter More Than IQ.* New York: Bantam Books, 1995.

———, ed. *Healing Emotions: Conversations with the Dalai Lama on Mindfulness, Emotions, and Health.* Boston, MA: Shambhala, 1997.

Hay, Louise. *You Can Heal Your Life.* Carlsbad, CA: Hay House, 1999.

Iacoboni, Marco. *Mirroring People: The Science of Empathy and How We Connect with Others.* New York: Farrar, Straus & Giroux, 2008.

LeDoux, Joseph. *The Emotional Brain: The Mysterious Underpinnings of Emotional Life.* New York: Touchstone Books, 1998.

McLaren, Karla. *The Art of Empathy: A Complete Guide to Life's Most Essential Skill.* Boulder, CO: Sounds True, 2013.

Mesich, Kyra, PsyD. *The Sensitive Person's Survival Guide: An Alternative Health Answer to Emotional Sensitivity & Depression.* Lincoln, NE: iUniverse, 2000.

———. *The Strength of Sensitivity: Understanding Empathy for a Life of Emotional Peace & Balance.* Woodbury, MN: Llewellyn, 2016.

Myss, Caroline, PhD. *Anatomy of the Spirit: The Seven Stages of Power and Healing.* New York: Three Rivers Press, 1996.

Orloff, Judith, MD. *Emotional Freedom: Liberate Yourself from Negative Emotions and Transform Your Life.* New York: Three Rivers Press, 2010.

———. *The Empath's Survival Guide: Life Strategies for Sensitive People.* Boulder, CO: Sounds True, 2017.

Penczak, Christopher. *The Witch's Shield: Protection Magick and Psychic Self-Defense.* St. Paul, MN: Llewellyn, 2004.

Ram Dass. *Be Here Now.* New York: Crown Publishing, 1978.

Rifkin, Jeremy. *The Empathic Civilization: The Race to Global Consciousness in a World in Crisis.* New York: Jeremy P. Tarcher /Penguin, 2010.

Rosetree, Rose. *Empowered by Empathy: 25 Ways to Fly in Spirit.* Sterling, VA: Women's Intuition Worldwide, 2001.

Segal, Jeanne, PhD. *Raising Your Emotional Intelligence: A Hands-On Program for Harnessing the Power of Your Instincts and Emotions.* New York: Henry Holt and Company, 1997.

Turner, Jonathan H. *On the Origins of Human Emotions: A Sociological Inquiry into the Evolution of Human Affect.* Stanford, CA: Stanford University Press, 2000.

**Opus Aima Obscuræ (OAO)** is the nonprofit multicultural temple, farm, and community center created by Raven Digitalis and by Priestess/Oracle Estha McNevin in Missoula, Montana.

**Mission Statement:**
**To serve as a ceremonial space and resource center**
**for the study of global earth-based spirituality**
**by offering a creative multicultural environment**
**for the practice of public ritual, humanities education,**
**and community-supported agriculture.**

The organization offers between five and fifteen public events on a monthly basis, depending on the season. Regular hands-on educational workshops include activities such as organic gardening, sustainable agriculture, animal husbandry, old-world cooking, international/holiday baking, cross-cultural arts, candle making, soap making, canning, food preservation, camping retreats, children's events, global tea service, beading, weaving, sewing, divination, yoga, healing practices, herbalism, and ongoing educational courses. As an organization rooted in both Neopaganism and Shaktism, OAO observes traditional sabbat rituals as well as a number of ancient Hindu festivals.

As a 501(c)(3) nonprofit charitable organization, OAO relies on donations, support, and contributions from the greater community. Private support is consistently needed and is deeply appreciated. Please contact the organization if you would like to receive paperwork outlining the organization's activities, outreach, and suggestions for support. All contributions are tax-deductible.

You may also contact the temple to be added to the virtual newsletter list, to receive seasonal care packages, or to inquire about professional services. These services include spiritual consultation, tarot reading, mediumship, past-life regression, and assistance with personal magick.

It is the goal of the organization to uphold a loving community, to help empower individuals, to compassionately provide educational opportunities, and to help make the world a better place one day at a time.

Namaste and Blessed Be!

**Opus Aima Obscuræ**
(OAO Temple Haus)
PO Box 2666
Missoula, MT 59806 USA
temple@opusaimaobscurae.org
www.opusaimaobscurae.org
www.facebook.com/opusaimaobscurae

## To Write to the Author

If you wish to contact the author or would like more information about this book, please write to the author in care of Llewellyn Worldwide Ltd. and we will forward your request. Both the author and the publisher appreciate hearing from you and learning of your enjoyment of this book and how it has helped you. Llewellyn Worldwide Ltd. cannot guarantee that every letter written to the author can be answered, but all will be forwarded. Please write to:

Raven Digitalis
℅ Llewellyn Worldwide
2143 Wooddale Drive
Woodbury, MN 55125-2989

Please enclose a self-addressed stamped envelope for reply,
or $1.00 to cover costs. If outside the U.S.A., enclose
an international postal reply coupon.

Many of Llewellyn's authors have websites with additional information and resources. For more information, please visit our website at http://www.llewellyn.com.